PROVEN METHODS TO MANIFEST YOUR DESTINY & DREAM LIFE RIGHT NOW!

THE MANIFESTATION GUIDE ON HOW TO DESIGN YOUR BEST LIFE WITHIN SIX MONTHS WITHOUT FAILURE, FRUSTRATION & GIVING UP: SPIRITUAL ALIGNMENT, THE LAW OF ATTRACTION & MANIFESTING LOVE, MONEY, SUCCESS, AND EVEN MIRACLES

ELYSIA

CONTENTS

INTRODUCTION

 "Ask for what you want and be prepared to get it!"

— MAYA ANGELOU

We can't explore the subject of manifestation—and the power it has to bring you your heart's desires—without acknowledging that it is a controversial topic. Some religions believe that manifestation is downright sinful. Some people are convinced manifestation is an attempt to be God-like; to become the master of your life, while we should be living in greater obedience to God's will. Well, what if God's will for us is to have desires? Life is a gift, and our desires are what motivate us to make the most out of the life we've been given. If He wants us to send out positive energy, will that attract positive things rather than the negative waves that surround us when our lives are not the way we want them to be? What if the belief that manifestation is sinful is effectively claiming that we have the power to change God's plans for us? Wouldn't that be sinful in a certain regard; to think so little of God's power?

I didn't write this book to play judge on this matter. I am not taking your eternal fate into my hands. What I know, though, is that you wouldn't have decided to read this book if your life was perfect. The opportunities you are hoping for, such as the romantic partner to share your life with, the promotion, house, health, and financial status you want to have—these things are just not coming your way, regardless of how hard you try. Maybe you've seen the positive results of manifestation in the lives of others. Perhaps you've read manifestation stories and now you are ready to try it yourself.

It doesn't matter if you've turned to manifestation as your last resort in a state of hopelessness or if this is your first port of call to manifest the life you desire; the lessons are all the same. Your life is a direct reflection of every choice you make, every emotion you feel, and every thought you allow to occupy your mind. We are created with feelings, thoughts, and the freedom to choose. Why not choose the positive things? Is it a noble thing to be trapped in misery? Do you really think it's the right thing to do?

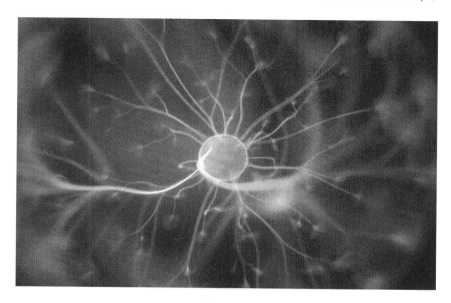

Another reality is that everything that exists on Earth comprises energy waves. You don't need an expert in manifestation to tell you that. When you read this in an article on manifestation, though, it is easy to make it out to be gibberish. However, if you read the same line in a science article, you believe it, right? There is no difference between the statements, the facts, and the truth that either reveal. It just takes a different perspective.

Another shocking realization regarding manifestation is that you are already doing it. You are already attracting specific energy toward you. You're just not content in life because you aren't doing it effectively, and so it isn't positive energy that you attract. When I say that it's time to change this around by manifesting effectively, in a manner where we will attract the things we desire, then it becomes a sin. Being happy is not a sin, being rich is not a sin, and being loved by the right person is not a sin. What it is, though, is living life fully; to enjoy life and the beautiful things in the world.

Now, you've bought this book, and you are reading it, which proves you are already committed to making a change. What are the benefits you can enjoy by applying the techniques I expand on in this book? Let me offer you some.

You will enjoy a greater level of optimism as you feel confident that you are going in the direction you want to be going.

You will experience greater confidence because you will compliment yourself, inspire yourself, and motivate yourself to do more, reach higher, and access greater achievements.

There is so much already written about stress and how it affects our mental, physical, and emotional states. When you use manifestation, you are reducing your stress levels and taking better care of yourself.

You'll feel increased gratitude. You'll realize the multitude of small blessings in your life, and expressing gratitude for them will become much easier.

WHO AM I?

I am Elysia. I am a music producer and a DJ, and I own a business. I am also the author of another book on manifestation. Since I was 12 years old, I have been studying the law of attraction. Yes, that was the age when I first had a dream of becoming a superstar DJ. Soon, my curiosity about manifestation paid off, and today I am living my dream life. I consider myself to be very fortunate for stumbling onto the power of manifestation so early in my life. I realized that I had tapped into a powerful source. It is a way to achieve your dreams, and the beauty of it is that it is available to everyone. So, I am spreading the word by talking about it, writing about it, and living it every day of my life. Therefore, I've written this book. Manifestation is a widely underutilized power source for improving the state of your life, without working your butt off and only reaping half of what you are supposed to be enjoying in life.

Employing manifestation doesn't mean that you don't have to do anything else to achieve your dreams. What I am saying is that, as you keep the wheels of your life rolling, manifestation will steer you in the right direction. You are on the journey of life already; you may as well make the most of it.

Several of the globe's most successful people swear by the positive impact manifestation has on their lives. I am sure Oprah Winfrey is the first name that popped into your head, but she is not alone. Ariana Grande and Lady Gaga are also massive fans of manifestation, employing the techniques in their lives and careers. Demi Lovato tweeted in 2010 that she would sing the national anthem at the Super Bowl. Ten years later, she was on stage realizing that dream she sent out a decade earlier (Nast, 2022).

My guess, my dear reader, is that you are tired, deflated, uninspired, and maybe even hopeless. You want that change you deserve, and you want it now. You will do what it takes to enjoy your breakthrough. You've put in the work and busted your butt for far too long, and now you want to reap the rewards of your efforts. But perhaps you are still cautious about manifestation, or even reserving your optimism.

Are you scared to proceed on this journey? Well, I want to share this quote from Marianne Williamson with you. May it be as inspiring to you as it was to me.

Our deepest fear is not that we are inadequate. Our deepest fear is that we are powerful beyond measure. It is our light, not our darkness, that most frightens us. We ask ourselves, Who am I to be brilliant, gorgeous, talented, fabulous? Actually, who are you not to be? You are a child of God. Your playing small doesn't serve the world. There's nothing enlightened about shrinking so that other people won't feel insecure around you. We are all meant to shine, as children do. —A Return to Love, 1996

On that note, don't be scared of what you are capable of.

Let's do this! Let's not waste a single second waiting any longer to steer your future in the right direction. Now is the perfect time to start manifesting your dreams and transforming your reality.

1

THE SCIENCE BEHIND YOUR CONNECTION WITH THE UNIVERSE

"Believe something and the Universe is on its way to being changed. Because you've changed, by believing. Once you've changed, other things start to follow. Isn't that the way it works?"

— DIANE DUANE

THE HUMAN BODY AND THE UNIVERSE

Change Is the Only Permanent Feature

Everything is connected. The entire universe—the cosmos, people, and creatures—are connected. Even when we zoom in on the minute details of our existence, we see that the cells in our bodies are all connected. More important, though, is that these things are all changing. Nothing is permanent. Death is constantly in our midst. But so are rebirth and renewal—they surround us and are inside of us. All the cells in our bodies are constantly dying and being replaced by new cells. This all happens with perfect timing. But this happens not only in our bodies—it happens in everything else too. Even the stars we see at night are in a constant cycle of change. They decay and release stardust and energy. This spreads throughout the entire cosmos and is absorbed by other living beings, reviving the energy, only to be released once again. Everything is connected through this spreading energy. The entire universe is in a constant cycle of renewal. Thus, the only certainty, and the only permanent state, is change.

What this teaches us is that life depends on death as much as death depends on life. We often refer to this cycle only as "life," but it requires both life and death to exist. Without the death of cells, there would be no space for cell rejuvenation to take place. There won't be growth, and once growth stops, death is taking place, for nothing is ever constant. Changes are always taking place.

As long as the body supports this process, renewal takes place. When the body cannot renew and cannot follow the steps in the process, then death steps in, for those parts that are dead are no longer released into the universe as energy, and there is no room for renewal. This situation becomes so severe that the body reaches a point where it contains more death than life, and then the entire organism dies off and releases all its energy into the universe.

One of the biggest obstacles battled by those who are curious about manifestation is to understand how something that was previously part of a shining star in the heavens, can now be part of them. To grasp this, we need to break down our existence to the most minute form. The entire universe comprises the following building blocks: "...the elements hydrogen, oxygen, carbon, and nitrogen—dominating in all life on Earth—make up over 96% of our body weight" (Schrijiver & Schrijiver, 2015). Where does this come from?

The sun's energy originates from nuclear fusions within the core of the sun, turning into a mass of light, which then travels to Earth to support plant growth. Plants absorb this energy and store it in their cells, only to release it once consumed by humans or the animals which humans eat. The carbon present in the human body comes from the carbon in plants, present because of the plant's photosynthesis. The remainder of our high carbon count results from burning fossil fuels, releasing the carbon present in this material, and then it gets absorbed by the human body (Schrijiver & Schrijiver, 2015).

The connection we have with the entire universe is further supported by the fact that 99% of the human body comprises the 11 elements most widely found in the universe. The composition of chemicals and water in our cells closely resembles the composition of the water in the oceans covering more than half the Earth's surface. These are the elements that make it possible to breathe, digest, think, and feel. Without other life on Earth, humans would cease to exist.

Throughout time, change has been constantly taking place. Earth, animal life, the star constellations, and the human body have all evolved. The constant change supports evolution by adapting to the changing conditions of our environment. When we explore the structure of atoms, it becomes evident that "atoms link us to the fast cosmic rays from deep within the galaxy" (Schrijiver & Schrijiver, 2015). Each of these atoms entering the human body contains elements that previously existed within the body of another being. It is all a cycle of death, recycling, and renewal.

Where did it all come from? As we come to understand that everything comprises the same elements; that the same building blocks supporting life as we know it come together to make one thing, we also need to understand where these elements come from. Where did they originate? As ages went by, "[…] nuclear fusion in the cores of the stars transform[ed] hydrogen and helium into progressively heavier elements. All elements in our bodies heavier than hydrogen were formed by nuclear fusion inside stars" (Schrijiver & Schrijiver, 2015). When stars grow old, they release more of their weight into the galaxy. Eventually, these particles reach the Earth's atmosphere where we inhale them or consume them through the plant or animal matter we eat.

These elements also gather in the galaxy, where they collide with each other, attach, and eventually reach the Earth's surface as a cascade of billions of particles. Earth is constantly showered with small pieces of broken-down stars. We gather the dust of the decay of the galaxy, but this decay is very much life-giving and loaded with energy.

The sun's existence depends on constant gas explosions that are loaded with magnetic energy. When the gas from these storms, resulting from the sun's explosions, reaches Earth, it causes geometric storms. This dust settles on the surface of the Earth and enters every form of life in existence.

What is the Earth? It is our home; the only planet where life is known to currently exist. But it is so much more too. When you build a house made of mud bricks, you may have created a place that you refer to as home. It can be the perfect habitat for reproducing and raising a family. Yet, the home is far more than that. Every brick contains elements of the soil where you gathered the mud. It is the footprint of all events that took place on that spot; the dust that settled there. In these bricks, in which you find familiarity as they come together to form this united whole you call home, you'll find trace elements of matter from faraway places. As you live in this home, you inhale these elements, touch these elements, and the dust particles can fall into your food and you consume these elements. It is all connected. Nothing within the borders of the world we know or in the widely unknown beyond is standing alone. It is all connected.

You are not only living in the world—you are part of it. Your body consists of the same elements as the world. Nothing separates you from it. Through this inherent connection, you can impact the world known to you, just as it affects you.

THE CONNECTION STRENGTHENS

The strength of the connections binding us all together is not stagnant. Just like how everything else in the universe is constantly changing, so are these connections. We contribute to the strength of the connection between ourselves and everything else in the universe through the following three steps.

Gazing

By living with an awareness of our surroundings and gazing at the world around us, we become more aware of this connection that ties us to the much larger network of life. This awareness occurs when we realize that the life we are living is no more than sharing the same space and time in a much greater plan of existence.

Knowing

Humans seek understanding, and through understanding, we can form new ideas which we apply to other objects in the universe. Through this interaction with other parts of the greater network, we strengthen the ties connecting it all.

Identifying

Once we become more aware of the existence of other living beings and that we are all connected through the elements present in everything, we identify ourselves not only as unique beings, but also as beings connected to the greater network of the universe, thus strengthening this bond (Wang, 2016).

Over recent years, more studies have revealed this inherent connection that ties us all together, not only with other people and living beings, but also with the greater cosmos. In 2019, doctors Guy Consolmagno, Jennifer Wiseman, and

David Charbonneau released a short documentary sharing their findings. Their research indicated that deep inside our bodies, we have elements that the stars forged during the process of transformation. Every part of the galaxy is constantly changing, transforming, and rejuvenating, and in this process, particles of its being are discarded, moving through the cosmos, ending up on the surface of other stars or objects, including Earth. Here we live and consume, and it is how we absorb elements contributing to our sense of belonging to this network (taotiadmin, 2019).

WE ARE THE CONNECTIONS WE MAKE

Each generation, just like each preceding one, has a fascination with the stars. We spend evenings looking at the stars, wondering about their existence. There has always been this attraction toward the stars and a desire to understand more about their existence. This longing is fueled by the connection we have with them. It is the longing we have to strengthen our bond with that which is beyond our reach, and yet woven into who we are.

Who is pushing to strengthen this bond? Is it the universe urging us to support a stronger connection, anchoring us in this existence? Is it the spirit that calls upon us by strengthening this desire to belong through the connection? Do we need to know who or what is encouraging the connection or urging us to seek ways to strengthen the connection?

By enjoying a closer connection, we enjoy greater assimilation with the universe. We access a larger source of energy. Energy is never destroyed, because it never ceases to exist. It transforms, and channels from one being to another. Thus, when we have a stronger connection with this network, we access a greater source of energy, which supports us in our ventures.

CONNECTING WITH THE UNIVERSE

How can we strengthen our connection? Can we even strengthen this connection? The following steps can help us enjoy greater connectivity with the network we belong to.

Being Still

The life we are used to is completely consumed by distractions. It thrives on these distractions, as it is through them that we attract our attention to accessing our intentions, thoughts, and eventually actions. We are living in a world and a time where being still doesn't happen organically anymore. Distraction never ceases to exist or to demand. If you want to enjoy a greater connection, you need to make a conscious effort to quiet your mind and soul.

Being still demands that you remain in the present. Notice your breathing; your being. Find a spot where you can be undisturbed. Ground yourself by finding a comfortable position with your feet on the ground. Notice how the air you breathe passes in and out of your airways. Breathe slowly and deeply, and find your natural rhythm. Spend a little time in complete harmony with the heartbeat of the greater network you are connected to by default.

Notice Your Internal Rhythm

The human body, just like all other living beings, has a unique internal rhythm determined by the pace of your heartbeat. Take note of this rhythm. Allow yourself to immerse in this constant and rhythmic beating. You will find that your body enters a new state of relaxation, allowing it to de-stress and connect with energy fields beyond your existence.

What Does Your Inner Voice Say?

The inner voice doesn't scream or shout, it whispers. You need to bring your body, mind, and soul into complete coherence with the vibrations of the external world in order to access your inner voice. Sit still, breathe deeply, take note of your heartbeat, and listen for the longings of your inner voice.

Recalibrate Your Vibrations

Everything in the universe is the same, but different. It all, including us, consists of the same collection of basic elements. It is merely the composition that differs. As we are the same, we belong, use, and allocate energy from this grid of energy. It also means that every cell in our bodies is charged, vibrating according to a certain resonance. Research indicates that the Schumann Resonance is the frequency of the Earth's electromagnetic field. It is essentially the heartbeat of the Earth. When we calibrate ourselves to this rhythm, we are on the same wavelength as the Earth's heartbeat. This strengthens our connection; it supports our existence. By spending quiet time in nature, this calibration takes place organically.

Express Yourself

Once you've reached a state of complete coherence with the heartbeat of the Earth, when you are grounded to its surface, the blockages inside of you disappear and your energy can flow freely. This opens your mind to identify what you are yearning for beyond recognition. In this state, you must express your intentions, deepest desires, and needs. By doing so, you are sending this energy into a vast cosmos charged with an immense capacity to deliver, as expected.

Finding Authenticity in Your Desires

You can't only express what you desire, you need to feel it too. Claim it with every part of your being—this is about accepting what you are about to receive before you've received it. Before the baby is born, parents prepare the nursery. Just so, you must prepare yourself to receive what you've asked for as if you've already received it. Be excited about it even before it has materialized in your life.

Align Yourself With the Universe

Once you've aligned yourself, placing your heartbeat with Earth's heartbeat and your energy waves with that of the surrounding cosmos, your connection opens up and expands to a much deeper level.

Do So Regularly

You can't expect results if you're not tapping into the energy source you are connected with regularly. Just like a car needs to make regular stops for fuel and batteries need to charge often, you, too, need to follow through in your intention to strengthen your connection, with regular efforts to make this connection stronger (Hall, n.d.).

Expressing Your Desires

Imagine you are sitting in a restaurant and want the server to bring you a refill on your coffee. The server is a bit preoccupied, as the place is extremely busy and thus hasn't had a chance to check in with you recently. The only way to get what you want, a refill on your coffee, is to attract his attention and express your desire for having another cup. You may have to wait for a little, and if he is very overwhelmed with serving other tables, you may have to ask for it again. Eventually, though, you will get what you want.

Another scenario would be when you are on the subway. You don't have a watch, but need to know the time to see if you are going to be late for an appointment. There are only a few passengers on the train. You notice a young man sitting a few seats away from you, deeply immersed in a book. As he is holding the book up, you spot the watch on his wrist. Now you know he can give you what you want, the time. So, you excuse yourself for interrupting him and ask if he can give you the time, please. He does, smiles, and continues with his book. You expressed your desire and got what you wanted. Problem solved.

If it is so easy in a world where we have limited beliefs about what we are capable of, why do we find it so much harder to express our desires, and send this request into the large network of energy that we are connected to?

One way to express your desires is through journaling. Writing is a far more powerful way of expression. It involves thinking about what you want to say, seeing the words you are writing, going through the physical movement of writing, feeling the pen in your hand and the texture of the paper as your hand slides over the page, and putting the words in your head down onto the page while you hear yourself saying them in your mind. Writing entails a much more comprehensive process than speaking, which is why journaling is such a powerful tool to express your desires.

For the best results, determine exactly what you desire. Then, by journaling these desires clearly and concisely, you send this energy, the desire for something, into the network of energy you are linked to. It is how you strengthen your connection with the network.

Believe What You Want to Receive Is Already Coming Your Way

I want to revert here to the expectant parents. They haven't seen their newborn yet. They don't have any certainty that the child will be born healthy and be coming home with them soon. They just believe, and by believing, they act as if they are already receiving. Sure, you can say that they have a sonogram to confirm the baby's existence, and even aside from that, they can see how the mother's belly is growing. Yes, there are signs, but there are also often signs to show us that what we've asked for is coming. We just need to become more in touch with our network to see these signs (Phillips, n.d.).

Maintain a Positive Outlook

Like attracts like. We attract what we reflect. If you are going to allow your mind to venture down paths of negativity, you'll likely attract more negativity into your life. Therefore, if you want to attract positivity, you need to radiate a positive mindset. So, even if it is extremely challenging at times, try to remain positive as much as you can (Phillips, n.d.).

Be Grateful

One way that makes it easy to radiate positivity is to focus on the things in life that you are grateful for. Consider each time you say "thank you" as a deposit into your savings account with the cosmos. Gratitude for what you have makes it easier to ask for more and to express your desires.

Program Your Subconscious Mind

The subconscious mind is a powerful force pulling the strings in the background. When you are excited about a new venture or challenge you want to take on, but soon after are hit with a multitude of reasons this would never work, you can be sure it is your subconscious mind that sits behind it all (Phillips, n.d.).

I want to explain a bit about how the subconscious mind works. Every day, you make a lot of decisions. What you will wear, eat, do, what time you will get up, whether you go out with friends or not—these are only just some decisions you have to make regularly, and as you constantly think them all through, your mind quickly becomes overworked. It also causes a lot of wasted energy. So, for certain things, your conscious mind relies on your subconscious mind to make decisions, in order to save energy. This is, in most cases, a helpful feature to have, but it can also mean that the subconscious mind will decide in the same manner every time, as it has determined the choice to be a safe option. If you've always done this action in a certain manner, this part of your brain will only repeat what it is used to. If you want to change it, you need to program the subconscious mind to think differently.

You can do this by locking into your subconscious mind right before bedtime. Try to think about what you desire for about five minutes until you fall asleep. This way, your desire will linger internally, strengthening it and increasing the energy to attract this desire.

Do the inner work before you sleep. What I am saying is, if you are already working so hard and not getting the results you desire, what do you have to lose by trying this effortless but powerful exercise?

It is time that we all drop the idea that it is 'us against the world.' We need to start seeing ourselves as part of a much larger network to which we are constantly contributing. What you deposit into this pool of energy is what you will be able to withdraw when you want to get what you desire. So, change the deposits you are making into positive ones, and reap the rewards in all areas of your life.

SPIRITUAL JOURNALING

I've mentioned how much power journaling holds in transforming your future. So, let's delve a little deeper into the topic of spiritual journaling, as this would be the first step I want you to take on this path of transformation.

> *"Journaling allows us to connect with our wisdom and creativity... The process serves as a useful tool for bringing insight and heightened awareness to ourselves and our lives."*
>
> — LUDWIG, 2021

Are you ready to journal? There are a few different kinds of journaling I want to explore.

Gratitude Journal

I think the most widely known journaling method is the gratitude journal. Here, you would capture even the tiniest little details of your day that you are thankful for. Maybe it is the fun moment you had with your cat as it chased a feather. Perhaps it's having a cup of hot chocolate when you are cold after a long commute home. Think of all the things you have and jot them down. This exercise is extremely helpful for lifting your mood and increasing your overall level of happiness in life. A good choice to change the energy deposits you've been making from negative to positive.

Intention Journal

An intention journal would be one where you jot down the goals you set for yourself. By writing down the things you want to achieve in life, you send your intentions into the universe to attract the energy you need in order to do it, but you also make a declaration to yourself. This transforms the intention, giving it more shape and direction.

Reflection Journal

While an intention journal focuses on what you want to achieve in the future, a reflection journal allows the opportunity to explore what you have already achieved and what else you would still like to achieve in your life. This way, you can identify where you need to place your focus, and what is still important enough that you want to achieve it. Through these reflections and the observations you make, you jot the pathway to your future.

Poetry Journal

How can you reach in and touch the deepest parts of your being? A poetry journal is a helpful aid to achieve this. You might not be a poet, but if you are not planning on becoming a published poet, then it doesn't matter if you identify as a poet or not, for this journal is only for you. Poetry connects people with parts of their being that they rarely consider. It enables you to reach deep down into your being, grasping even those parts that you so seldom attend to.

Dream Journal

I love dreaming. I love it because it is a way to escape everyday life, but it also helps to visualize the life I desire and gives me a taste of what it would feel like to live that life. Dreaming strengthens our desires, allowing our visualizations of the life we want to become more vivid and closer to reality. All the while, dreaming also contributes to making our dreams our reality. Keeping a dream journal can also help you to have a record of the many things you once desired that are now part of your life.

Which of these journals appeals to you the most? Are you ready to pop out to the stationery store and invest in a pen and a journal in order to complete the picture? Do so now.

FINAL THOUGHTS

When I chose to start this book, and specifically this journey with this chapter, it required a lot of thought. I understand that often, you might feel so tired and hopeless that you are only seeking the solutions that will bring you relief, but I didn't want to give that to you straight away. I wanted you to first grasp why manifestation works, how your existence links in with the universe, and how you are connected to forces much larger than yourself. I had to make sure that you grasp how your existence is always changing, just like how the universe is always changing, and that we are all connected. I can't just say so without presenting you with the research and facts to show you that there is a lot of evidence to back up my claims.

Now that we've done that, we are moving on to finding spiritual alignment. What is this, you ask? What does it feel like and how can you achieve this in your life? Read on.

2

SPIRITUAL ALIGNMENT

When we are experiencing moments of despair; of feeling frustrated with our current situation that seems to be the theme song of our lives. It is often a very lonely place. It may feel as if you are all alone and nothing and nobody favors you and your dreams or goals.

I was experiencing such a moment myself once. In that moment, I felt that nobody believed in my dream to become this amazing DJ. It felt as if people dismissed my dream and, in a way, they did, for nobody can truly share the same emotions over the future you've envisioned for yourself as you do, and rightfully so. Every person must make their own dreams a priority—not yours. In the same manner, you must make your dreams a priority and not expect others to do it. Still, it was an extremely isolated place for me to be in. I was without inspiration and didn't feel like it was worthwhile to continue trying. During these moments, we feel trapped in our assumptions that regardless of what we do, it will not bring the outcome we desire. So, we fill our hours, days, and even weeks with loads of insignificant things to consume our attention. It is once we've lost our focus on the bigger picture for our lives that we fill moments of boredom with getting lost on social media. Then, as I was scrolling on one of these platforms that became my go-to place when I wanted to escape my life, I saw a quote by Amit Ray. He is a well-known author and spiritual master, teaching yoga and meditation, as well as a powerful advocate for peace and compassion. The quote read: "You are never alone. You are eternally connected with everyone." —Amit Ray

Those words jumped right at me. Then, I realized that if I am connected to everyone, even with all elements in the universe, and I don't feel that connection, my priority should be to strengthen the connection so that I can move in alignment with the greater force I am connected to. This connection is the spiritual connection. It is what we are going to explore in greater depth now. What is a spiritual connection, and how can you strengthen this connection to allow a free flow of energy and enjoy spiritual alignment?

WHAT IS SPIRITUAL ALIGNMENT?

The best comparison I can come up with to express the concept of spiritual alignment is to compare it with a car. Cars and their complexities are familiar objects to most. So, let's consider this: Picture yourself behind the steering wheel of a car, as you head off into the sunset. The car runs smoothly while all the parts in the car are in perfect alignment. When one piston goes up, another goes down, ensuring you have a smooth journey. You are not even aware of the engine's components, and for as long as that all runs well, you have no interest in looking at what is going on beneath the hood. When one part starts to move out of its alignment, you can be sure to have car problems. The engine won't be running optimally, and if it goes unattended, you will have some major car concerns. The lack of effectiveness in one part of the car puts additional strain on another, resulting in it wearing out or even breaking down.

The same is true for spiritual alignment. If you are not aligned with the greater force, network, or universal system you are part of, you are bound to have some struggles that will leave you feeling isolated. If you are out of spiritual alignment, there are parts of your being that will experience additional stress, causing it to malfunction. As we progress through this chapter, you will notice what are the most common symptoms of not being spiritually aligned, and be able to identify if this is a concern to you.

Alignment is in place when your entire being is moving in the same direction. When you are focused and moving with purpose and intention, you feel a sense of contentment and of being strong and confident. It might be that the obstacles between you and your goals are still massive, but you have the sureness that it is the way to go, and you feel empowered to overcome these challenges.

Being in spiritual alignment will cause you to feel connected to the higher source, to a power beyond your abilities. Even in the face of challenges, you can still enjoy an inner state of happiness and peace. Experiencing a state of spiritual alignment is more than a mere state of being. It is also about doing what needs to be done, keeping the wheels rolling in the right direction. Eckhart Tolle explains this, as he says, "When the basis of your actions is inner alignment with the present moment, your actions become empowered by the intelligence of life itself." (Stone, 2021).

The sense of being spiritually aligned encompasses your mind or heart, as it takes over every part of your being. In these moments, you are aware of the plan that is in place for you, that your goals—which appear to be so enormous—don't even compare with the wonder, beauty, and success that are reserved for you. This, in turn, leaves you with a sense of acceptance, knowing that it is not only you who are working toward greatness in your life, but that you can count on the support of your connection. You are becoming aware and appreciative of the fact that it is an effort made by the entire universe that you belong to and are aligned with.

How do you refer to the divine force you believe in? Regardless of whether you call it God, the universe, or Mother Earth, it is not about the name you prefer to use; it is about acknowledging your connection with the divine force and knowing you are not alone in your quest for greatness.

Signs You're Out of Alignment

Maybe you are not entirely sure where you are at. Maybe you are out of alignment or never have been aligned, and therefore have no idea what the feeling is that I am talking about. The following are all symptoms of being out of alignment, causing you to vibrate on a different wavelength than the system you belong to:

You Feel the Pain

We are holistic beings comprising mind, body, and soul. All of these play a role in our state of being. Thus, if you are out of alignment, you are bound to experience symptoms in all of these three aspects of your being. Often, the physical is the first to give us signals, yet we choose to ignore these warning signs, as it is so easy to blame our symptoms on other causes. If you have pain in your knee, it might be that you are not feeling that you have the support you need. Furthermore, your muscles are stiff, causing a lack of energy flowing through your body, in turn caused by your vibration that is out of pace with the rest of the system.

You Drown the Pain in Alcohol

Alcohol makes us feel happy, relaxed, and empowered. I am not saying you are not allowed to drink, within limits. I am warning you, though, that if you notice that your alcohol consumption is increasing lately, you need to determine why you are searching so intently for those happy feelings inside a bottle, and why you can't seem to find them anywhere else. When your life is in such a state that it feels better to be intoxicated most of the time, you desperately need to make some changes.

Overindulging in Food

While some resort to alcohol in order to enjoy a sense of relaxation, a deeply rooted indulgence, and/or pleasure, others turn to food for this escape. It can be that your endless hunger is not to fill the void in your stomach, but your soul. You can't eat yourself happy. Sadly, this is not how the universe works, and while indulging in unhealthy foods and consuming unhealthy quantities may bring momentary relief, it often leads to more advanced long-term concerns. If you are indulging in food to silence that echo of loneliness inside, I want to encourage you to instead seek out the way to spiritual alignment. It is how you engage with the power available to you, just as it is to all. Let's shift our focus to fill the internal void through spiritual healing, and not through takeout.

Poor Sleeping

At nighttime, darkness enhances our fears and uncertainties. It multiplies all the things we feel we lack, while casting a shadow of doubt over all that is good in our lives. This is when our minds run off in the wrong direction, keeping us from vital sleep. When we are sleeping, our bodies are mostly in overdrive to restore, renew, and replenish. It is also when we refresh our minds and turn a new page on the emotional challenges we experienced the previous day. Instead of grabbing artificial solutions to resolve your insomnia, why not restore your spiritual alignment? This way, your sleep will be beneficial to your overall well-being.

We Receive What We Reflect

Being stuck in traffic is nobody's choice. Yet, there are days when other drivers seem to have it in for us. Have you experienced days when more people will cut you off, take your parking space, or even give you the finger? Remember, negative energy attracts more negative energy. The same rule applies to the positive energy you radiate. Thus, if you find yourself often to be the victim of others' poor behavior, you might just benefit from exploring what you are sending into the universe. Rather than pinpointing the negativity, rudeness, or hostility you may experience from others, try to turn toward internal reflection and determine how your mindset has contributed to the situation.

Anxiety, Lack of Focus, and More

All the symptoms I've mentioned so far show that your spiritual alignment is out of sync with your energy force. If you lack sleep, you are bound to feel tired more often, and struggle to focus. This can lead to increased anxiety, fear, and even depression. The idea of being stuck in a hopeless situation is often enough to leave anyone sick to their stomach. Another way to express this is to visualize a group doing line dancing. Imagine one person is not hearing the same music or rhythm as the others. There are going to be moments when you bump into them, and this can lead to frustration and anger. Nobody is right, but nobody is wrong either. You are just not connected, moving at the same rhythm, pace, nor do you have optimal timing.

The Manner In Which You Present Yourself

One of the most influential forms of self-representation is the manner in which we speak. The words you use, the way you use them, and the body language that you fall back onto, all make a statement about who you are, what your level of education is, what values you live by, and much more. Have you ever spent time in a conversation where one person is constantly swearing? Did you feel completely dragged down and drained afterward? Of course you did, for your vibrations matched theirs. Compare this experience to someone who speaks in an upbeat manner, and communicates with clarity and focus while using an impeccable vocabulary. Now you have a sense of how vibrations affect your being. When you are not aligned with the greater force, it is often visible in the way you speak and the language you naturally lean toward, like cursing or using negative or demeaning words.

Your Breathing Is Rapid and Shallow

When someone is in a state of deep relaxation and contentment, their breathing is slow and deep. Every breath is loaded with life-giving oxygen that enters the body and disperses to where it is needed. If your breathing is shallow and rapid, your entire being is in a state of feeling threatened and alone. This happens when we feel vulnerable. Watch your breathing, as it will indicate where your overall state of being is at.

Lack of Motivation

Is your obsession with the tiniest details holding you back? Do you know what you need to do, but you simply can't find the motivation to do it? A lack of motivation is another signal that your spiritual alignment is out of sync. Then, we allow procrastination to take control of our lives.

You Present a Fake Version of Yourself

Are you afraid that once the world you are familiar with sees your authentic colors, it will reject you? Mock you? Humiliate you? Spiritual alignment brings about contentment with who you are. It increases the level of appreciation you experience for the person you've become, your skills, and all the special attributes that contribute to your uniqueness. Thus, if you are hiding your true self and always living a lie, it is a sure sign that your alignment is out of sync.

The Need to Control

While I was still in school, I had a close friend who was bulimic. She trusted me, and would often share what she was going through mentally and emotionally—even how much she hated herself for not being able to stop. She always stated that she felt her life was chaotic, and that vomiting was the one thing she had control over. She could decide when she was going to do it and when to stop. For her, it felt like control, but it was no more than an illusion of control, for she couldn't stop at all. When our lives are running out of control, it is only human to seek areas where we might have more control, and then employ every effort to maintain control over this one insignificant area. Do you hang on desperately to a certain person, relationship, circumstance, or expectation simply because you believe it allows you to have some control? This is not what control looks like. For how long, still, do you want to hold on to an inferior life when brilliance is awaiting you? Let it go.

HOW TO RESTORE SPIRITUAL ALIGNMENT

Now, we've covered in enough detail what it looks like when you are not in spiritual alignment. So what do you need to do to restore this state? I will expand on several steps you can take to help you in this regard, but essentially it all boils down to unblocking your internal energy flow in order to allow the energy and support of the universe to enter and run through you. You'll know deep down when you are not spiritually aligned. I want to move on to how to unblock yourself in every part of your existence.

For restoring and maintaining your spiritual alignment, it is important to take note that this is not a one-off exercise, where once you've completed every step, you will remain aligned for life. No, this is a connection that you need to maintain in order to enjoy its optimal benefits.

Let's visit our car comparison one last time. You have to maintain your car by refueling it regularly, taking it for service, checking the tire pressure, and making sure all four wheels are aligned and in balance. However, none of these things are meant to be done only once. To ensure your car runs optimally for as long as possible, you need to take these actions often. These steps I am sharing should also become habits for sustaining your spiritual connection.

Be Grateful

Shifting your thoughts to focus on all you have, and not all you lack, brings an immediate sense of relief. However, there is much more to gratitude than making you feel better about life. Several studies over recent years have been exploring the immensely positive impact that gratitude has on our lives, including a reduction in depression and anxiety. This is even the case for those who are struggling with diagnosed mental illnesses. In one 12-week study, researchers explored the impact of gratitude in combination with counseling, and the results showed that those who applied gratitude along with counseling enjoyed far better results than the groups relying only on counseling or on showing gratitude (Brown & Wong, 2017).

Gratitude is a way to shed any toxic emotions holding you down. Even if you don't externally express your gratitude, you will reap the benefits. This is why a gratitude journal is such a helpful aid in improving your spiritual alignment. Don't expect the changes to take place in your life immediately, but know that the impact of gratitude on your being—

and especially your brain—is lasting. This was proven by the previous study, as after 12 weeks, scans showed a change in the brain structure of those who regularly showed gratitude (Brown & Wong, 2017).

There are many ways you can show your gratitude, apart from keeping a gratitude journal. Write someone a thank-you letter and mail it to them. Give someone a gift unexpectedly. Pay it forward. Do some good by leaving positive energy in the world.

Pray More

Prayer is so often misunderstood and widely undervalued. A prayer is a form of direct communication with God. It entails that you open a communication channel and reach out to the power invested in Him, a force so strong the entire universe depends on it. While anyone can pray, this is a practice widely linked with Christianity, as prayer is essentially a conversation with God. Yet, even though prayer is so often linked to the Christian religion, so many Christians ignore prayer completely and opt instead to make quiet desperation part of their journey. Wouldn't harnessing the power of prayer and communicating with God be an example of exemplifying His works in your life?

The Bible states humans are composed of mind, body, and spirit. While the body is our vehicle during our life on Earth, we remain spiritual beings. Through this connection between our spirit and the Holy Spirit, we gain greater access to God and it becomes easier to live our lives according to His master plan. Pray, for it will restore your connection with God and bring you back to spiritual alignment.

Eat Healthy Food to Feed Your Soul

The food we eat shouldn't only replenish our bodies, but also feed our souls. We can't expect food that is overly processed and contains high loads of preservatives and artificial ingredients to nourish our souls when it is not even good for our bodies. Certain foods we consume bring about several benefits. Typically, primary foods are considered soul food. These are foods that are still in their rawest form and are organically produced. These include foods like raw vegetables and fruits, nuts and berries, and whole grains.

Yet, good food contributes so much more to the soul when it is consumed with love, appreciation, and gratitude; when our meals become celebrations of life rather than a quick bite on the run. Meals mean more when we eat good food while being mindful of what we eat.

When you eat, make sure you taste the different flavors, feel the textures, and immerse yourself in the aromas. Don't just bite into an apple in between meetings. Take a few minutes and look at the red flecks on the apple's skin. Enjoy the crunch when your teeth settle into the sweet flesh. Taste the sweetness with a touch of acidity; the apple's essence. This way, every meal will not only still your physical hunger, but also ease your emotional starvation.

Value Your Time

We all have 24 hours in the day. Every hour is 60 minutes long, and every minute is 60 seconds. With time, we all start on an even slate. Yet, some have time and others don't. Is it perhaps because you don't value your time? Are you keeping busy with things that don't immerse your being or contribute to realizing your dreams? Maybe you are bored and waste time on other insignificant things just to get time to go by. Do you long for Friday, and pray that Monday and the start of another work week just don't come?

We live in an age of believing the lie that the more we are busy in multiple places, the more we become omnipresent and productive. This is not the case at all. The more things we are involved in at once, the less present we are anywhere, as our minds are occupied by constantly shifting focus and never truly attending to the necessary details.

This is exhausting, to say the least. Strive to become present in one task at a time. Immerse yourself completely in that task and reduce the amount of stress you experience at any given time, and you'll find that you get through all the tasks on your to-do list faster.

This will require, at times, that you ignore certain distractions. It will require you to sometimes close your door and switch off your computer or your phone. Maybe you have to physically remove yourself from your situation, or the environment you are in. The golden key to creating the life you desire is to get rid of those things that you don't want in your life. If your many possessions are consuming your life to the degree that you don't have time for yourself, then that is what you need to let go of. The clutter in our world, our minds, and even on our desks are mere obstacles preventing our spiritual alignment from remaining in an optimal state.

Rest Regularly

Without proper sleep, our bodies, minds, and souls deteriorate. This is why sleep is such a widely studied subject. A lack of quality sleep increases our stress levels, and anxiety brings along several physical ailments and leaves us emotionally vulnerable. A lack of sleep negatively impacts our work, our ability to focus, the state of our relationships, and our health. When we sleep, our body rids itself of toxins, allocates less energy to digestion, and has more resources available to take care of cell renewal and recovery. While this takes place in the physical part of our being, our minds get to detox. During every moment you are awake, your mind is bombarded by stimuli from the world you live in. This becomes clutter in your mind, and without granting the time needed to clear the clutter, this, like the clutter on your desk, becomes an obstacle to your efforts to enjoy spiritual alignment. So, make sure that you get enough sleep regularly.

Simplify Your Life

We allow ourselves to become so immersed in matters that appear to be so important. It is so easy to become trapped in the web of complexities in our relationships, career, emotions, and even our possessions. Spiritual alignment operates on the concept of less is more. The less you have to fill your life, the more time you will have to live your life filled with the things you want. So, clear your life of the drama, the toxic relationships, the things you don't need, and the people who contribute nothing to your life. Clear the path for the energy you seek, allowing it to flow through you in order to set your passion alight and guide you in the right direction. This will help you get your spiritual rhythm aligned with the rhythm of the force you belong to.

Meditate Regularly

Meditation is an active effort to still your mind and increase your focus. Meditation helps you to manage your stress levels and to gain new perspectives on the matters that are of concern to you. It also raises your level of creativity and makes you more aware of your connection to other parts of the universe.

If there is one thing on this list of steps that will make a difference in your life, and the outcomes you enjoy, then it is meditation.

Exercise

You don't have to be a fitness fanatic to reap the many benefits of exercise and its ability to help you become more spiritually aligned. Try a walk in the park or anywhere in nature. Allow yourself the time to take note of the sounds, the images, and the scents of your surroundings. Notice the sensation the breeze leaves on your skin, or how it plays with your hair.

Find your connection through physical movement. It may be yoga or another form of exercise that allows you to clear blockages in your mind and heart, and as you increase your heart rate, you will feel liberated and hopeful.

When you exercise, exercise with intent. What do you want to achieve? While exercising, listen to what your body is telling you. Take a mental scan of any discomfort, pain, or stiffness you experience. Stretch to become more flexible, allowing energy to get into every part of your existence.

When we seek a path that will take us to stronger spiritual alignment, we often need to simplify our lives and clear them of the unnecessary clutter that obstructs the connection we desire. Are you ready to spring clean, to allow the energy in?

THE FIRST STEP IN SEEKING SPIRITUAL ALIGNMENT

When you are ready to let go of the obstacles in your way, the following statements will guide you on your way to spiritual alignment:

- I will seek help. Who can you ask for help when you realize that you are too often claiming control, even in situations that aren't good for you? Seek out those who can share their wisdom with you and support you on your journey.
- I will answer my curiosity. Is there any specific part of the spiritual journey that stands out for you and which you want to expand your knowledge on? Identify where you'll be able to learn more and find the answers you are seeking.
- I will take breaks in nature. Take midday walks in nature and refresh your perspective. After a short midday walk, you will feel refreshed, revitalized, and ready to give your best for the rest of your day. Schedule time to take breaks.
- I will capture my thoughts. Write down your thoughts, ideas, and dreams. Remember, you write this for yourself and no one else. You are writing this purely for your benefit and have the freedom to write whatever you feel like.

- I will set boundaries. When do you stop people from entering your life and wasting your time? When do you begin to put yourself first? You have to put boundaries in place to protect what is yours.
- I will let go. More important, though, is that I will realize what is already gone while I might still be holding on to it.
- I will breathe. Take time to breathe, allow fresh air in and exhale toxins from your body, toxic thoughts from your mind, and toxic people from your life.
- I will check in with myself. Your emotional, physical, and mental state is important. Make sure that you are aware if anything is off and take the necessary action.
- I will determine what my values are. Who do you want to be? What are the values you want to surround yourself with? Who are the people you want to spend time with and eventually become more like?
- I will invest in myself daily. If you don't value yourself enough to invest in yourself, how can you expect others to invest in you? Other people often follow your lead in the way they treat you. If you value yourself, they will too. If you are confident in your abilities, you will win the confidence of others as well (Matejko, 2019).

CAPTURE THE CURRENT STATE OF YOUR SPIRITUAL ALIGNMENT

It is time to reflect. In your journal, share your ideas with the universe about the current state of your spiritual alignment by providing honest answers to the following questions:

- What pain am I experiencing? What is the root of this pain?
- Who do I need to forgive to set myself free?
- What obstacles are preventing spiritual alignment in my life?
- How can I change my perspective to overcome these challenges?
- What are the things in my life I don't like?
- When and how can I free myself from their presence?
- With what would I want to replace these?
- What is my purpose in life?
- What is preventing me from fulfilling my purpose?

FINAL THOUGHTS

In this chapter, we've discussed spiritual alignment, the power it holds, and what is possibly keeping you from enjoying this connection optimally. Obstacles that prevent you from enjoying the full benefit of alignment with the universal force you are connected to can take on many forms. However, most often. these obstacles are present in one area of your existence, while affecting several other areas too.

As you would want to attract more of the positive and less of the negative, we need to explore the principles of the law of attraction. We will do this in the next chapter.

3

LAW OF ATTRACTION

Like attracts like. What you put out into the world will reflect on you. I've touched on this concept already, but to fully harness the power and possibilities available to all by employing the law of attraction, we need to explore it in much greater depth.

Buddha said, "All that we are is the result of what we have thought. The mind is everything. What we think we become." (*Gautama Buddha*, n.d.).

As I've often found that many people approach exploring the law of attraction with a lot of doubt, I thought it might be helpful to bust some doubts with facts about this phenomenon and how it has grown in popularity.

- During the late 1990s, which isn't that long ago, statistics showed that a mere 2% of the adult population believed in the law of attraction. Today, just over 20 years later, the number has grown substantially, with 73% of the adult population believing this law to be true.
- This growth surge was largely due to the release of *The Secret*. The book, by Rhonda Byrne, provides readers with nuggets of information to help them employ the power of the law of attraction in their own lives. *The Secret* was exactly what readers, starving for self-improvement and validation, were seeking, and it became an international bestseller.
- The industry serving this belief, providing content to help those keen to explore it in greater depth, has experienced an upward growth curve of 6-11% over recent years. This is an industry valued at around $776 million. Do you still think that the law of attraction is nothing but gibberish? There are enough people out in the world valuing this law to spend that amount of money on becoming familiar with its finer details, and learning how to reap the benefits it offers (LOA Admin, 2022).

THE HISTORY OF THE LAW OF ATTRACTION

At the core of its existence, the law of attraction is merely the belief that you will have more of what you focus on the most. If it is wealth that consumes your mind, you will have more of that, but if it is your lack of wealth that is overshadowing your mind, then you are bound to find yourself immersed in poverty. Age, gender, culture, or even religious belief does not influence this law. It is considered a universal law, and whether or not you acknowledge its existence, the reality remains that it will impact your life. Thus, as it is a law that opens itself to contributing positively to your life, why not use it?

Many centuries ago, it was initially believed that the law of attraction was only a Buddhist teaching. Eventually, it took on the name 'karma' which spread across all barriers into a globally used term. Yet, when we closely study the Bible, we'll find mention of the same law in several verses there, too, indicating that the law of attraction is not limited to any specific group, but globally applies to all.

By way of exploring documentation that reflects the impact of this law on the lives of many, throughout generations, it is evident that many famous names in history had a lot to say about the power of this law. Shakespeare, Newton, and Beethoven are only some of the many names appearing on this list. While it's hard to accept that the law exists if your life is in shambles, I urge you to instead seek how you can employ the law to your benefit, rather than try to dismiss its existence.

More recently, the law has also become a subject in the world of quantum physics and, through research, we can now understand more about how mind attraction works (*What Is the Law of Attraction? Open Your Eyes to a World of Endless Possibilities*, n.d.). However, you don't have to understand the deeper details and science behind this ancient law in order to employ the benefits it can bring to your life. A bit later on, we will hear what experts in quantum physics have to say about the phenomenon.

WHAT IS THE LAW OF ATTRACTION?

Before we proceed, I want to establish an understanding of how to define the law of attraction. The law of attraction is rooted in the philosophy that positive thoughts lead to positive outcomes. It is a phenomenon that occurs because thoughts are a form of energy, and when you have positive thoughts, you are reflecting positive energy, which attracts more of its kind. The same rule applies to negative thoughts, attracting negative energy. It is important to understand that there are no scientific facts to confirm these observations, but as it is a philosophy so widely understood and appreciated, the law of attraction has earned a rightful position as a pseudoscience.

When we take an even closer look at what it entails, we notice it comprises three principles. These are:

Like Attracts Like

In life, we favor people and situations that we are familiar with. It is much easier to build rapport with people who share our ideals, dreams, viewpoints, and goals. There is even the proverb "Birds of a feather flock together," which is based on the understanding that people who are similar are attracted to each other. It is a natural rule surpassing human nature, as it applies to all other elements in the universe too.

The same rule applies to our thoughts. If we are constantly immersed in negative thoughts and expectations, we are bound to attract more negative energy into our lives through negative experiences and unsuccessful outcomes. When we make the conscious choice to focus on all that is positive, we attract positive outcomes and experiences.

Nature Abhors a Vacuum

This situation summarizes the second stage of transitioning from a negative state to the maintenance of a positive outlook on life. Nature doesn't allow for any empty spaces. The laws of physics simply don't allow for it to happen. If you remove something from an enclosed space, it will always fill up with something else, even if that is merely air. Compare your thoughts with an enclosed space filled with negativity. When you take deliberate action to change the type of thoughts you host and push negativity out of your mind, it is bound to be filled with something else. The only alternative here is positivity. Nature won't allow for a vacuum in your mind. So, by pushing out negativity, nature automatically fills your mind with positivity.

The Present Moment Is Perfect

One of the biggest challenges humanity faces is to free ourselves from the inclination to persistently wander off in our minds into the past or the future. Instead of being present in the moment, we punish ourselves over regrets for things that took place in the past, or we provide room in our thoughts for anxiety about the future. While drifting off in either direction can be very consuming and will leave you emotionally charged, it is a completely fruitless situation and a waste of energy. When we focus on the present moment and how we can optimally utilize the moment we are in, we are making a valuable contribution to the future, which then also becomes far less anxiety-provoking.

Energy is expensive and we should be discerning in the manner in which we utilize this resource. The most effective manner in which to go about with your limited resource of energy is to focus on the present, making the best of your current situation. Automatically, this will positively impact your future too.

HOW TO USE THE LAW OF ATTRACTION TO YOUR BENEFIT

Understanding what the law of attraction entails is one thing; knowing how to use it to your advantage is another. If you want to optimize the benefits of this law in your life, we have to explore how you can use it to manifest your dreams.

The Law of Attraction and Finding Love

We all have desires of the heart. For many, this desire is to find love and someone to share their lives with as they grow older. It is impossible to attach value to the enriching experience of sharing your life with someone you cherish and who, in return, adores you for who you are.

To receive love, you need to open yourself up to attract the love you deserve. Increased confidence and charisma are only two of the contributing factors to help you attract the love and romance you desire.

To find your soulmate, you must be clear about your desire. Invest the time and effort needed to get to know yourself first, and make it evident to others and the universe that this is what you desire. By doing so, you are sending the type of energy that will attract what you are seeking in the area of love and romance.

The Law of Attraction and Money

Money means something different to everyone. We all have a different definition of what wealth means. Yet, when using the law of attraction, these differences don't matter, for you would want to attract wealth in terms of what it means to you. Sadly, though, many people are much more concerned with their lack of money than the abundance they enjoy already. The outcome then, of course, true to the nature of this law, is that you only attract greater poverty.

Instead, try to shift your mindset in order to focus on what you desire, and visualize having these things already in your life. Read articles about money. Learn all there is to know about making money. This is how you can change your approach to making money. Also, adjust your behavior to reflect abundance in your life. This way, you are attracting the energy that will get you the financial position you desire.

The Law of Attraction and Health

Whether it is greater physical or mental health you are seeking, there are several physical steps you need to take. Take care of what you eat and how active you are, and go for the necessary medical check-ups to ensure you are in excellent condition.

While enjoying excellent mental and physical health forms the foundation for having a happy and content life, it is not a guarantee that you'll have it. Many people enjoy an exceptional state of well-being, but still experience negativity and a sense of lack in this area of their lives. To counter this, shift your focus to what is positive and good in your life. Emphasize what you are grateful for and attract more of what inspires you to be happy.

The Law of Attraction and Success

As with wealth, the meaning of abundance and what success entails differs between people. To attract success, you need to define what would constitute success for you and what having abundance means to you. Does driving a sports car symbolize abundance to you? Maybe being your own boss is what you translate as success.

It doesn't matter, for only you can define what you want, how you will feel when you have it, and what you need to do to get there. Then, start to believe that you already have all these things, and immerse yourself in the positive emotions that surface when you do, to attract more of these feelings as support in manifesting your desires.

HOW DOES THE LAW OF ATTRACTION IMPACT YOUR LIFE?

When you are dealing with such a powerful phenomenon as the law of attraction, it is important to consider how it will impact your life on various levels. The two most prominent parts of our being affected by the law are our spiritual state and our physical well-being.

Impacting Your Spiritual Well-Being

When you are applying the law of attraction in your life, it is bound to impact your spiritual state. It is impossible to acknowledge the powerful influence of the law without acknowledging a higher power, which essentially requires that you are spiritually inclined. Utilizing the law demands greater awareness of the energy you radiate. It requires that you acknowledge that all is connected and that we are part of a much larger network.

By adapting your approach to life considering this greater awareness, you become happier, more content with life, and far less depressed, anxious, or stressed out. Soon, you'll find that the triggers sending you over the edge into emotional disarray lessen, and you'll have greater confidence to handle challenging situations with ease.

Impacting Your Physical Well-Being

Our existence can be defined as a complex network of interdependence between emotional, physical, and mental elements of our being. When you are emotionally distraught, the impact of this is bound to ripple out into other parts of your being. Stress and anxiety cause your physical health to deteriorate.

This ripple effect is also prevalent the other way around. If you take deliberate action to manifest certain improvements in your physical health, you are going to experience a positive impact on your mental and emotional state, too.

What this all boils down to is not only are we all connected to all else in the universe, but also every part of our being is connected. Everything impacts everything. While this idea might be daunting, it is a thought that has always excited me. See, when everything is connected, then change—even on a minuscule level—is bound to impact every other part of the system.

Say you want to manifest financial abundance and visualize that you already have this abundance. By doing so, your level of confidence is automatically increased. This confidence can cause you to take greater risks that bring about greater rewards, taking you closer to your goal. The success you enjoy causes your physical health to improve as you experience less stress, and as you are radiating positivity, you affect the entire system you are part of. It all works together, as it is all connected.

What Scientific Proof Do I Have?

Allow me to just dip my toe into the world of quantum physics for a minute. Before, I've said that there is no scientific proof to back up the law of attraction. While that is the case, experts in quantum physics are not oblivious to the impact of this law on the wider cosmos. The result is that when we explore the law of attraction from the angle of quantum physics, it is evident over time that the field of study delivered several plausible explanations. In this regard, I would like to quote the words of Max Planck, a Nobel Prize winner, and widely considered the father of quantum physics. He devoted his entire life to studying science based. Planck said:

> I can tell you as a result of my research about the atoms this much: There is no matter as such! All matter originates and exists only by virtue of a force that brings the particles of an atom to vibration and holds this most minute solar system of the atom together... We must assume behind this force is the existence of a conscious and intelligent Mind. This Mind is the matrix of all matter (Singh, 2020 para 6).

Taking his words into account, I think it is safe to say that humanity has been and still is underestimating and under-utilizing the power invested in us to transform our lives, manifest our desires, and impact the entire cosmos we belong to.

PRACTICAL STEPS TO EMPLOY THE POWER OF ATTRACTION

Up to this point, I've shared a wider perspective on how manifestation works by employing the law of attraction. I consider this to be vital information when you are serious about exploring the inherent power we all have, and you want to know how to optimally use your power. Now, I want us to get more practical by taking a step away from theory and scientific explanations. Let's walk through the steps that will help you benefit from the law of attraction in your life. After all, humanity still operates from the principle of "seeing is believing" and I want you to see the benefits of manifestation in your life, just like I've experienced it firsthand.

Visualize Your Life

Do you know what you want in life? I've often found that people are more inclined to tell me what they don't like about their lives, and can identify the element(s) they want to get rid of rather than having clarity on what they want.

You need to make the time investment to determine what you want. Be clear on every aspect of your life that you want to improve. Understand that the more you visualize this, and the greater the detail with which you visualize it, the more likely it is to become your reality. Before moving on to the larger goals you want to manifest, why not start with something small? Visualize enjoying a productive and successful day. Take stock of your success at night before going to bed and decide for yourself if it works for you. Remember, the more you train your brain to become accustomed to visualizations, the more power your visualization will have and the greater its influence on your life will be.

Keep Your Eye on the Goal

Do you want to hear a fun fact about race car drivers? They speed around the track at immensely high speeds. How do they manage to do that? Simply by keeping their eyes on where they want to go. Taking their focus away from the road, whether to look at the audience or another driver, can cost them the race and, even worse, their lives.

The same goes for tennis. The perfect serve is not one where you kept your eye on the ball, but when you maintained your focus on that spot where you intended the ball to hit the court. You will always go to the point where your gaze is focused. This is why you need to know your goals. Write them down in as much detail as possible and never take your focus off these goals. Don't look at what others are doing, for this will only slow down your progress. Know your goals and maintain your focus on them.

Affirmations - Employing the Power of the Verbal Word

When was the last time someone told you how capable you are? Can you even remember the last time you complimented yourself? While affirmations are a powerful way to boost your confidence and attract positive things into your life, most people feel uncomfortable complimenting themselves out loud.

I want you to experience the power of affirmations and to enjoy the sense of accomplishment it establishes in life. So, I urge you to find a statement that is clear and direct and say it aloud to yourself. Look in the mirror and stare into your own eyes. Connect with the person you see in the reflection and tell them that today will be a magnificent day, or that they can accomplish anything they set their mind to.

If this is too daunting, there is an alternative you can try. Record yourself making these affirmations, and when you are on the subway or have time to spare, put in your earphones and listen to your voice, making these statements and affirming the power you have inside of you.

Learn All About the Law of Attraction

When you love someone, you get to know every part of their being. You become an expert on their facial expressions, words, and reactions. You even grasp what they are truly feeling just by listening to the tone of their voice. The more we familiarize ourselves with anything in life, the more we absorb it into our being. If you want the law of attraction to become an integral part of your being, you need to learn everything there is to know about it. Don't stick to one article or one source of information. Read several opinions and learn all the finer details there are to know, and that is how you assimilate this power into your life.

Sharpen Your Focus Through Meditation

Contrary to the belief of those who haven't meditated, meditation is not a process during which you clear your mind of all thoughts, but rather a time during which you focus only on one specific thing. Meditation forces the mind to quiet down and, during this time, it will be beneficial to shift your focus to one specific goal you want to achieve. It is during this time of stillness that you can connect your intentions and your innermost desires to manifest the life you dream about.

Be Kind to Yourself

It is so easy to be kind to others while we are extremely harsh on ourselves. I once read an article that suggested this occurs because when we look other people in the eyes, we can see their souls, but we don't ever look ourselves in the eyes. The article then urged the reader to spend about five minutes in front of the mirror, just looking into the eyes of their reflection. It was a completely new experience for me and I just had to try it. I was completely overwhelmed by the deep sense of compassion that came over me. Initially, it was a rather unusual experience, but I simply allowed this experience to filter through me. It is much easier to be as kind to yourself as you are toward others once you've looked yourself in the eyes. Then it becomes easier to do what is necessary to manifest your desires.

Be a Beacon of Positivity

You don't need me to tell you that the predominant energy we radiate in this beautiful world we call home is negative. Not only are far more people—in general—negatively inclined, but negative energy is also far more contagious than positive energy. The world needs more people who simply spread positive energy. You can do this by being kind, patient, caring, and compassionate to others. Share the good that is happening in your life and celebrate the joy others have to share.

Monitor Your Progress

You can keep track of the progress you've made by sharing the highlights of your day with your loved ones. You can also keep a record of how you are getting closer to your goals by keeping a journal. Your journal will become the record of your progress, giving you a reference to see how far you've come on those days when it is harder to remain naturally upbeat.

Stay Committed to Your Gratitude Journal

This point is closely linked with the previous one, as a gratitude journal can also serve as a record of how you are progressing. By using a gratitude journal wherein you can express gratitude for all you have, you shift your focus toward the positive, as well as toward where you are heading in life. Please don't ever slow down your progress by slacking on this journal.

THE MISTAKES I'VE MADE ALONG THE WAY

Progress often happens amid bumps and disappointments. I am sharing some mistakes I've made along my journey simply because I didn't know better. Now I do, and when we know better, we can do better. I also want you to be aware of these mistakes in order to prevent them from slowing your progress down.

I Didn't Know What I Wanted

I've said that you need to be clear on what your goals are, and now, I am emphasizing this point again. One of the greatest mistakes everyone makes when they want to manifest a better life is being uncertain about what they want.

I Wanted Too Much Too Soon

When we start a fitness regime, most people know you can't just jump right in and start by jogging several miles on the first day. No, it takes time to prepare your body for the enormous challenges. Yet, when we look at manifestation and use the law of attraction, we want to manifest big things right away. This is not how it works. Manifestation is a process you need to get better at. Rather than immediately going after something big, break this big goal down into smaller steps and manifest each of these steps first. This is how you gradually move closer to your goal and gain confidence that the network you are part of will support you.

Don't Root Your Desires in Negativity

It took me a while to realize the law of attraction works when our desire is rooted in things in our current existence, which we want more of. It should not originate in efforts to avoid the things we don't like. Don't link your desires to such negativity. If you do, it will be impossible to shift your focus away from the things you want to remove from your life.

You Are Not a Victim

The best thing I did for myself is realize that I am not a victim of my circumstances, but that I am in control of my life, and if my life is not what I want it to be, then I need to manage my life better. I believe at any moment, our lives are a direct reflection of every choice we've ever made. By accepting that responsibility, you set yourself free to move forward.

Your Desires and Purpose Aren't Aligned

Know your purpose and make sure that whatever you desire —and want to manifest using the law of attraction—is aligned with it. Everything you do needs to be aligned with your higher purpose, otherwise, it just won't work out.

You Have Contradictory Emotions

Sometimes we are our own worst enemies. This happens when we desire something, and go as far as to affirm our desires and our dreams to the universe, but what we don't admit is that we are internally conflicted about what we ask. Say you desire to be wealthy and you express this desire, but internally, you experience conflict, as you view wealthy people as arrogant and self-obsessed. You cannot manifest your desire until you've resolved your perspective on wealthy people.

Other Mistakes...

Remember, I've been studying and using manifestation in my life for more than a decade, so the list of mistakes I have made is quite comprehensive. Besides the mistakes mentioned thus far, I've also had to learn:

- I have to be consistent in expressing my desires. Manifestation and using the law of attraction should never be a half-hearted effort, that you only do when you remember it.
- Manifestation is a tool to support the action you are taking. You can't sit back and wait for your dreams to become reality without taking action on your side.
- Enjoy the journey instead of obsessing about the outcome. During manifestation, we also go through a lot of transformation, and that is part of the journey. Enjoy the process.
- As transformation is part of the journey, you can't reject change. Open your mind and your being to accept change as a form of growth.
- Take note of changes to yourself, your emotions, thoughts, and ideas. This way, you'll notice even the most insignificant changes taking place inside, encouraging you to do more.

PRACTICING THE LAW OF ATTRACTION AT HOME

The best way to familiarize yourself with the powerful impact the law of attraction can have on your life is to practice it. As you are now more familiar with what you should and shouldn't do to enjoy optimal results, it is time to get practical. The following are a few exercises you can do at home to get you going on your journey of manifestation, by trusting in the law of attraction:

Create Your Dream Board

You can call it a dream board, a visualization board, or any other name you like, but essentially it would have to include visual triggers of the things you want to enjoy in your life.

Employ free will and personal choice and claim this board to express your deepest desires. By creating this board, you will also gain greater clarity on what you want and who you want to be.

Daily Affirmations

Do you still feel awkward about telling your reflection how wonderful it is? Then embrace the discomfort that's accompanying your growth. Decide what it is you want to tell yourself. Create a clear and direct statement capturing its essence and commit to affirming this to yourself daily.

Have Fun with the Future

One type of journaling I haven't mentioned yet is a future journal. Pick a time in the future, maybe six months or a year from now. Visualize what you want your life to be like then, and create journal entries as if this is your life at the moment. Another option is to write a letter from your future self to your present self. What would it be like to live the life you desire? There is no right or wrong way of doing this. Just make sure you have fun doing it.

FINAL THOUGHTS

Manifestation and the law of attraction are inseparable. In this chapter, I've provided you with a basic understanding of what the law of attraction entails and how you can use it to your advantage. We've explored how you can optimally use it to manifest your dreams, and what mistakes I've made along the way. Yet, the best way to familiarize yourself with the law of attraction and become confident in using it to manifest your dreams is through practice. So, without further delay, jump in and take on any of the previously mentioned practical exercises explained above. Next, we will put the term 'manifestation' under the microscope.

4

MANIFESTATION

Napoleon Hill said, "Keep your mind fixed on what you want in life: not on what you don't want." (Thought for the Day, 2017). Like most quotes, this sounds so inspiring, but what does it mean in real life? Let me share a story of someone just like you who manifested her dreams by using the law of attraction.

Nadia Simpson was an average student when she had her introduction to manifestation and the benefits it can bring. She shared a story of how her older brother introduced her to the film *The Secret: Dare to Dream,* based on Rhonda Byrne's book of the same name mentioned earlier, and how much it inspired her. She watched it on many nights during her first year at university. By the start of her second year, she created a vision board reflecting her dreams and goals. She stated that she pinned pictures on this board that represented her short- and long-term goals. This inspired her to start her own business, and one of her goals was to get a feature in Forbes magazine. So Nadia pinned a picture of Forbes magazine on her board. At that stage, she didn't have a network and there was no way for her to get this kind of coverage. Still, she believed it would happen. Gradually, she started attending networking meetings and then she met a Forbes contributor to whom she could pitch her business. The biggest lesson she learned is that she had to think less about how she was going to achieve her dreams, while believing more that she can get what she wants, and that she could create her reality (O'Connell, 2022). Nadia's business was featured in Forbes magazine on March 8th, 2021.

WHAT IS MANIFESTATION?

I define manifestation using the words of Rhonda Byrne, the woman who made manifestation a popular term. She says, "Manifestation is the art of intentionally attracting something that you desire into your life." (How to Manifest Desires, 2022).

But there is more to this definition. Manifestation depends on the law of attraction, and the most important attribute of manifestation is that it is unlimited and you can manifest anything you want in your life. Even if you are not actively trying to manifest anything through the natural law of attraction, you will still manifest those things by which your thoughts are mostly consumed.

Therefore, when our thoughts are mostly leaning on the negative, our lives comprise facing one obstacle after another. What makes manifestation an art, is that we can just as well make the conscious decision to focus our thoughts on the positive things in life and benefit from this law. Transforming your thoughts from being predominantly negative to being positive is an art.

As we've discovered in the previous chapter, the law of attraction is one of 12 universal laws, functioning from the principle of like attracts like. So you will always have more of those things you ponder the most. If it is your dreams, you manifest that, but the same holds true if you are constantly pondering your fears. Essentially, the law of manifestation is the tool for how you can manifest your deepest desires.

BUSTING MISCONCEPTIONS ABOUT MANIFESTATION

To truly comprehend what the term manifestation entails, we also need to consider what manifestation is not, even though some of these ideas are widely believed.

Manifesting is not all you need to transform your dreams into reality. Just imagine how easy it would be if we could all just sit back and dream, and while we are doing that, our dreams turn into reality. This sounds too good to be true, because it is. By relying on the law of attraction, you can manifest things into your life, but it still requires that you take action too (Regan, 2022).

Manifesting Is an Easy Way to Achieve Your Dreams

If it is such a foolproof and easy way to get everything your heart desires, why isn't everyone doing just that? Many people fail in their efforts to manifest simply because what they want is not aligned with their purpose, nor is it for the greater good of the world.

Another reason many enjoy no success through manifesting is that, while they send out positive energy with their conscious minds, the subconscious mind remains doubtful. Believe with your entire being and you will receive what you desire (Regan, 2022).

Manifesting Delivers Your Dreams as Ordered

Have you ever heard the saying "Be careful what you wish for"? It is almost the same scenario as manifesting your dreams. You don't always get what you've asked for in the exact manner you've requested. What I think, though, is that sometimes what we get is even better than what we've asked for. However, just know that how the universe manifests desires might sometimes differ from what you've pictured (Regan, 2022).

MANIFESTATION WORKS!

Now that we've busted these myths, I am so excited to share how manifestation works, as it does indeed work regardless of whether you notice it.

As I am sure some readers have a greater need for information on the science behind manifestation, let's delve into some facts.

The Reticular Activating System

Our brains are bombarded with stimuli and triggers every second of every day. If we had to process every piece of information entering our minds, our brains would be completely overworked. So, there is a safety mechanism acting as a filter to prevent some stimuli from entering. These filters shape our reality and viewpoints in life, and they are constantly evolving. These filters are very real and rooted in a part of the brain called the "reticular activating system." When you can sit in a noisy coffee shop and remain focused on the book you are reading, your reticular activating system is in an excellent state. It filters out all the background noise to help your brain remain productive (Kate, n.d.).

The Observer Effect

This brings me to the second point of interest, namely the Observer Effect. The Observer Effect is linked to a study known as the Double Slit Experiment. It is widely publicized, and I urge you to read up on it more. The Observer Effect claims that by observing something or someone, you change the portrayed behavior. Take yourself, for example. How does your behavior differ when you realize someone is watching you? Simply by observing what you are doing, that person affects your behavior and the outcome of your actions.

To further expand on this effect, when someone looks at you critically, your behavior will change differently than when someone is looking at you lovingly. So, how someone observes your behavior impacts the outcome of your actions.

Now, let's change positions around. Can you see how if you are observing your life, your dreams, the world, or anything else in a positive light, you will positively impact the outcome? Conversely, when you observe it negatively, the outcome will be less desirable (Kate, n.d.).

The Law of Assumption

This ties in with the law of assumption, stating that everything you believe or assume to be true will become true. So, by assuming that something will happen, you influence the outcome. If you always assume that the worst will happen, then that will be your reality. If the power lies within, why don't more people change their assumptions and positively impact the outcome? Because they don't believe they have the power to change the state of their lives.

Cognitive Bias

The last point I want to make here is about cognitive bias, another scientific term. Cognitive bias is a systematic pattern of deviation, allowing everyone to create a subjective reality based on their personal opinions. You can spot cognitive bias when two people observe the same scenario but have different versions of the story. To both parties, what they state they saw is very real, and both can be right. Both will also refuse to admit that what they saw might not have been exactly accurate, for once the brain decides on its viewpoint, there is truly no changing its mind. We all have a unique cognitive bias, as this is shaped by our life experiences, events, education, and upbringing, to name only a few of the contributing factors (Kate, n.d.).

Can you see that manifestation is not simply magic? Every aspect of manifestation is based on a scientific explanation. Yet, while science supports the phenomenon, so many people struggle to believe in the effect it has, as their belief systems don't hold space for this kind of thinking.

Quantum Physics and Manifestation

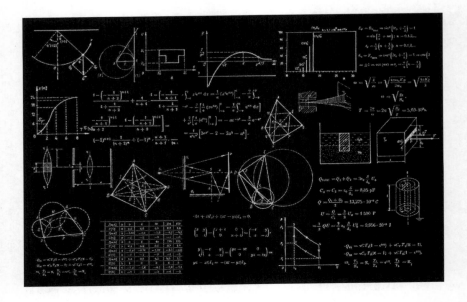

Quantum theory states that the world consists of atoms. Each atom is interchangeable and is charged with energy. This means that atoms impact each other, and the number of ways in which they can cause a change in each other is endless. The law of attraction states that thoughts are like atoms, as they also have an energy charge and can generate power. As all matter and thoughts are charged with energy and are interchangeable, our thoughts can impact matter and shape our reality in this way.

This is how the world of science provides scientific facts and observations to back up the concept of manifestation, taking it from being mere magic to an actual scientific phenomenon (Warren & Amir, n.d.).

HOW TO MANIFEST

Understanding the science behind manifestation can be complex. Fortunately, employing the effects of manifestation in your life is much easier. Following these steps will help you shape your reality by using manifestation to your benefit.

Gain Clarity on What You Want to Manifest

Effective manifestation requires a clear message. Thus, for as long as you remain vague about your dreams and desires, you will endure a poor outcome. Spend some time defining exactly what you want for your life. When you know what it is, write it down in simple terms and then visualize how it will feel when it becomes your reality.

Adjust Your Mindset

The beliefs that determine your life have developed over time and often result from circumstances beyond your control. You might not even have been aware these beliefs existed, or known the impact they have on your life. Now, you know better and you can change your mindset to benefit you. Identify what beliefs are holding you back and how you can overcome these beliefs, so you can set yourself free to achieve your goals.

Don't Just Dream It, Do It

You have a dream, but as long as it doesn't have a plan attached to it, it will always remain only a dream. Manifestation doesn't work on its own—you need to take action to make things happen too. Put a plan in place and become active in working toward realizing what you desire.

Be Grateful

Be grateful for what you have, but also for what you have yet to receive. You can employ gratitude to switch your mindset from being immersed in lack to enjoying abundance. Practicing gratitude can seem like an insignificant act, but it plays an immense role in your spiritual journey.

Change Your Vibration

You are familiar with the concept that we are all operating according to vibrations. The vibrations we are sending into the universe determine the vibrations we receive back. If you want to change the type of vibrations you receive, you need to change your vibrations first. Simple, practical ways to achieve this are meditation, yoga, and exercise. Also, make sure that you get enough sleep, that you are constantly working on improving yourself, and that you're eating healthy food.

Open Yourself Up to Possibility

For energy to flow through you and recharge you, you need to allow it in. While you remain in a state of negativity, you are blocking the free flow of energy, but once you open yourself up, you are bound to find yourself in the right place at the right time with the right people to manifest your goals.

Manifesting Is Who You Become

If you want to become fit, you need to spend a certain amount of time exercising. When you want to become an excellent DJ, you must spend many hours behind the deck. But when you want to become excellent at manifesting your dreams, it requires more than merely spending a set amount of time per day on this exercise. "Manifesting is a self-development practice to live by. It is a way of living." (O'Malley, 2022, para 25).

It means that everything you do, from the thoughts you think most about, your behavior, and your relationships, are all influenced by your desire to manifest your dreams.

Manifestation in a Nutshell

We can talk for hours about manifestation, moving from the most inspiring success stories to the most complex scientific explanations. However, I don't think understanding how manifestation works is as important as simply knowing that it does, indeed, work. I also don't think it is as important to know the number of other people whom it has worked for—it's best to stay focused on how you, too, can manifest your dreams.

Always remember that manifestation comprises only three steps:

- Ask for what you want clearly and directly.
- Believe that you are going to receive it.
- Receive what you've asked for with gratitude.

THE 12 UNIVERSAL LAWS

You are now familiar with the law of attraction and the law of assumption. I've mentioned that there are 12 universal laws, and it will be beneficial to expand slightly on these laws.

The Law of Divine Oneness

This law states that everything in the universe is connected. This law is the foundation of what I explained in depth in Chapter 1—that we are connected to everything in the universe.

The Law of Energy or Vibration

The entire universe is composed of vibrating atoms. These atoms move in a circular motion, and everything in the world, including our thoughts, has a unique frequency at which it vibrates. I will expand on this law slightly later on.

The Law of Action

The foundation of this law states that every action we take delivers a different outcome. Actions are not merely defined as physical actions, but also as our thoughts. Thus, by changing our actions or thoughts, we create a different outcome.

The Law of Correspondence

"This law states that we are in control of our life. Every action we make will be reflected in our outer world to our inner world." (Phooi, 2018).

The Law of Cause and Effect

Nothing in life happens merely by accident. Coincidence doesn't exist, as this law states that everything happens for a reason, even when we are not aware of the reason at the specific time.

The Law of Compensation

Throughout our lives, we receive money, gifts, blessings, friendship, and more. This is the compensation that comes because of the law of cause and effect.

The Law of Attraction

I think we've covered this law in enough depth for now.

The Law of Perpetual Transmutation of Energy

As we have the power to control the frequency at which our thoughts vibrate, we hold the power to impact our situation and circumstances in life. Therefore, we have the power to use our energy to transform our lives.

The Law of Relativity

Life is not always easy. There are many challenges that we have to overcome as part of our journey and how we grow as individuals. This law requires that we compare our problems and challenges with those which others face, so that we can realize the fact that others might be in much worse situations.

The Law of Polarity

What this law confirms is that when things go up in life, they must come down again. We can't acknowledge the negative things in our lives without acknowledging the positive too. Everything in life has an opposite.

The Law of Rhythm

Energy operates on vibration, and these vibrations form a pattern or rhythm. "Everything has a cycle and stages of development. The only way to master each rhythm is by facing the negative part of each cycle." (Phooi, 2018, para 19).

The Law of Gender

This brings us to yin and yang. Everything in the universe has a gender. It can either be masculine (yang) or feminine (yin). Every person needs to find a balance between these two aspects of being.

The Law of Vibration

Everything in the cosmos vibrates on a unique frequency. This frequency differentiates objects and people. While you can't see the frequency, you can sense it, and without even noticing that you are doing it, react to this frequency too. When you become more aware of your frequency, you will note what influences your frequency negatively and what has a positive impact on it. As you can change your frequency by changing your actions, which include your thoughts, you can use it to your benefit.

WAYS TO EMPLOY YOUR VIBRATION TO YOUR BENEFIT

The three predominant ways you can benefit from adjusting your vibration are:

- To manifest your desires by adjusting your vibrations in a manner to attract the outcome you want.

- To navigate you through challenging situations by being aware of changes in your vibration, and what is having a positive or negative effect on your frequency.
- To manage your emotions, as these, too, are vibrating, and you can improve your emotional state by raising your vibrations. Lower vibrations are synonymous with sadness and fear, while joy, love, and other positive emotions vibrate at a higher frequency.

HOW TO RAISE YOUR VIBRATIONS

The best thing you can do for yourself is to value yourself enough to invest time and effort in taking care of all your needs.

- Self-care is vital for raising your vibration, and it will leave you feeling stronger and ready to approach life with confidence.
- Take care of your body by nurturing it through giving it time to rest, heal, and relax.
- What do you enjoy doing? Once you've found what makes you happy, make time to do more of that and reap the benefits of it in your life.
- Meditation is a trusted way to improve the frequency of your vibrations.

THE LAW OF ATTRACTION VERSUS THE LAW OF VIBRATION

While these two laws are very similar, they are not the same. The law of attraction only comes into play once you've employed the law of vibration to change the frequency you sent out into the universe. Once your vibration is optimal to attract a positive outcome, that is what you will attract.

A HELPFUL MANIFESTATION HACK

We live in a time when everything happens quickly. It is an age earmarked by instant gratification. Whatever you want to happen will happen, and it happens fast. From searching for something online to getting the takeout you ordered, this age has conditioned us to expect everything to happen fast— even our manifestations.

Yet, we can't set an exact time for when something should happen. It doesn't happen according to our timeline. Sometimes manifestation is in progress, but we don't see it until the very last minute. The hack that I am sharing will not change the way manifestations work, but from my experience, I would say it speeds up the process.

So, get a pen and paper, and simply start your first sentence with the words "I am certain..." Complete this sentence with what you want to manifest. Examples would be:

- I am certain I've met my target.
- I am certain I've met the love of my life.
- I am certain I have abundance.

Once you've captured your desires, immerse yourself in the feelings you'll enjoy when you have received what you wanted, and enjoy the impact of manifestation in your life (Kate, n.d.).

MANIFESTING AT HOME

There are more ways to manifest your desires than the hack I've shared above.

An excellent exercise to increase your financial state would be to shift your focus to your bank account. What is the balance you see when you check your statements? Can you see the number in your mind?

Yes? Good, now see it grow. Visualize how this number grows exponentially, and every time you look, there is more money in your bank account. Even after you've paid your bills, the amount continues to grow. Spend about 10 minutes on this exercise and remember the most important aspect is that you don't think about the work that would go into earning that money, as for now you only want to focus on a growing bank account.

You can do this with any desire you have. Maybe you want to manifest a car, a career, a romantic partner, or excellent health. Take 10 minutes a day and make it happen.

FINAL THOUGHTS

Manifestations are not magic. They don't require you to believe in magic. What they rely on is using the natural laws to your benefit. This means you need to explore the processes that are already taking place, the ways these laws are already shaping your life, and to use these laws to shape the life you desire.

Whether you acknowledge these natural laws or not, it won't impact them. Still, you have the freedom to change your approach, your perspectives, and your actions to employ these laws to your benefit.

5

MANIFESTING LOVE

"The instant we realign with love, the Universe responds powerfully. At any given moment, we can change our story and say yes to what we truly want. As soon as we do, the Universe delivers."

— GABRIELLE BERNSTEIN

We've covered all that was necessary for having a basic understanding of manifestation and how it works. Yet, knowledge doesn't mean a thing when you don't put it into practice. Therefore, across the next four chapters, I am zooming in on specific areas of life where most people employ manifestation to realize their dreams. We start with the most important aspect of life: love.

MANIFESTING LOVE

Whenever we manifest anything in life, the process requires that we send out a clearly defined expression of our desire into the universe. This is why we need to understand exactly what we are asking for. To manifest love, you need to understand the concept of true love first.

Love Doesn't Demand

True love accepts the other person unconditionally. Likewise, this other person should not expect you to become someone you are not. However, this doesn't mean that you both remain stagnant. Through true love, change takes place because you want to improve in order to be a better partner for the person you love.

Love Doesn't Complete You

It is such a cliché to say that your partner completes you. I am opposing this statement because it can directly be translated into stating that you are incomplete without the other person. I want to emphasize that you are already whole as a person—you are amazing and valuable and just perfect. Finding love adds to this, and having this person in your life complements your personality. You don't need to find someone to fix you or to make you better.

Love Just Happens

If you are unsure about a future with your current partner, you are most likely not experiencing true love. True love often steps into our lives during those moments when we least expect it, or in situations in which we didn't think we'd find it. Once you find it, you know this is meant to be.

Love Is About Give and Take

You can never just receive when you experience true love, just as you can never just be the one who gives. True love demands a relationship where both parties give equally, selflessly, and without keeping score. Giving in such a relationship is not motivated by the desire to be the one who always wants to give, nor is it motivated by being the one giving in order to have the 'right' to ask at a later stage. No, giving is inspired by a mutual desire to share the best you have with the other person.

You Need to Love Yourself First

If you can't love yourself and celebrate who you are, how can you expect anyone else to love you in this way? True love is ignited in the presence of self-love. Before you can love someone else, you have to know how to love yourself first.

WHAT DOES IT MEAN TO MANIFEST LOVE?

When you understand what it is you are manifesting, you must make sure to grasp the process of manifestation.

Setting Your Intention

What is the kind of love you desire? Before you can manifest love in your life, you need to be clear on what it is and what you want from it. Answer the following question to gain greater clarity on what it is you are asking for:

- Who is the person you want to share your life with?
- What are the characteristics you are seeking?

- What kind of partner do you want to be in a relationship? Perhaps someone fun, but reliable and supportive?
- What is the kind of relationship you desire to have?

Try to add as many details as possible to your answers. Remember, the universe requires clarity in all we manifest.

Believe You'll Get What You Want

Are you convinced that you deserve this kind of love? This is the most common obstacle people have to overcome. It is so easy to desire love, but we prevent this from happening as we are not truly convinced that we deserve it.

Remember the following:

- You might have made mistakes in the past, but we all deserve second chances. Claim yours.
- You are worthy of love, and while the entire world might have a certain opinion of you, through true love, your partner will love you for exactly who you are.

Immerse Yourself in Love

Love comes in many forms. While you are seeking true love romantically, make sure you are surrounding yourself with all the other types of love already present in your life, may this be the love of friends or family. In the same way that like attracts like, love attracts love, so make sure you are optimally placed to attract the love you desire.

MANIFESTING LOVE

What makes manifesting far easier than we think is following a few simple, practical steps to achieve what you want.

Make a List of What You Want

At the core of any manifestation is writing. It is easy to underestimate writing and the power we can access by putting our dreams into words. But you know better now, so the first step you need to take is to list all the things you desire from your relationship and your romantic partner.

Anchor Yourself to the Future

Once you've completed your list of the things you desire, write a letter to your future self, expressing this beautiful relationship you've manifested. Expand on what you are feeling, how your life has changed, and what your days look like now. Immerse yourself in the situation and put everything you feel, see, and experience into words.

Meditate on What You Want

The more you play out your future in your head as if you are watching a movie, the more it becomes real to you. Meditation offers the perfect opportunity to immerse yourself in this movie, in which you are the main character.

Always Remain Grateful

Don't only express gratitude for what you have already received, but also be grateful for what you are about to receive. There is no better time than today to be grateful for the beautiful relationship and the amazing partner whom you are going to meet. Gratitude for something that is going to happen optimizes the frequency of your vibrations to attract exactly what you seek.

ARE YOU CONCERNED YOU DO IT ALL WRONG?

It has happened a few times that people say to me, "Elysia, I just don't think I am doing it the right way. How will I know if I should be more patient or change the ways I use to manifest love?"

My answer usually is that the universe operates on the energy you radiate, and when your intention is pure and true, your vibration will bring you what you want to manifest and no practical step will override this. Yet, when it is still not happening for you, consider if you are guilty of the following:

- You aren't clear about what exactly you desire, so you are sending out mixed signals.
- You are not honest with yourself and there are still conflicting emotions running around beneath the surface. If this is the case, dig deeper and be honest with yourself.
- It could be that a self-limiting belief is holding you back. Can you identify this belief? Resolve this concern.
- Maybe you were not comprehensive enough in stating your goals and dreams. Try to add more detail to what you visualize and want to manifest.
- Is there any action you can take? If so, do it.

- Do you harbor fears lurking in the shadows? Fears vibrate on negative energy, so you need to clear the space by addressing your fears.
- Maybe you are getting signs, but aren't noticing them. Search for any signs you might have missed since you first started manifesting love. Don't ignore these signs. Things always happen for a reason, and you need to explore these moments in greater depth.

WHY ARE YOU STRUGGLING TO FIND LOVE?

When you are not getting what you want, you may have to go back to the drawing board to see where you are going wrong in manifesting the love you desire. It might be time to go through the process with a fine-tooth comb and see where you've erred or could simply perform better. Consider the following potential causes:

You've Shut Down and Don't Realize It

- How many times have you been hurt or disappointed by love?
- How many failed relationships are spread across your past?
- How often have you left partners bleeding in heartache, collateral damage, or a failed attempt to make a relationship work?

- How many times was your heart broken during these attempts?

If you answered "often" to the last question, then you need to ask yourself if you've shut down internally. Closing yourself off to love can be a gradual process or it can happen in an instant. It can be a conscious choice or a transformation you haven't even taken notice of. Yet, if it happens, you are blocking your attempts to manifest love, and you need to open your heart to love again and allow yourself to be vulnerable in seeking it (Hurst, 2017).

You Have Business That You Need to Take Care of First

How often do we go through life, desiring a new future where we have manifested everything our heart desires, but we keep one foot firmly planted in the past and in all we claim we don't want? The unfinished business in our lives can hold us back from improving our lives and bettering our futures. Maybe you are still burdened with hurt from a past failure, carrying resentment over how you've been treated, or maybe you haven't amputated a former partner from your life. Sometimes we hold on to a specific relationship as we see that person as some sort of "Plan B." In this scenario, you figure: "What if I don't find a partner ever? Then, at least, I can settle for this partner from my past, even though they aren't what I really desire." We only hold a back door open when we are not convinced that the right person will walk through the front door of our lives. You can't say that you trust in the power of manifestation while your plans are structured around doubt. Shed the doubt first. Break the ties to the past, and set yourself free to move forward (Hurst, 2017).

You've Lost Faith, and No Longer Believe You'll Find Love

Is your desire to manifest love diluted to more than a whimsical wish? Yes, you might jump through all the hoops and take all the actions in order to manifest love, but deep inside of you, you don't have faith any longer that you'll find love. While you might hide this belief from the observing eyes in the world, you can't be inauthentic with the vibrations you send into the universe. You won't enjoy success if you don't believe you'll get what you ask (Hurst, 2017).

The Person You Want Isn't Available

Sometimes it is not necessarily love that we want to manifest, but rather the love of a specific person. Do you already have someone in mind and have that person pictured as your ideal partner, as the only person you want to love you? If so, you might just have stepped onto controversial territory. While you need to be specific about what you want to manifest, it won't be to your benefit to prescribe to the force of the universe what you want in such a particular way. Maybe that person is not available. Remember, you only receive as long as what you are asking is working toward a greater good.

You Believe You Don't Deserve to Be Loved

Do you want to be loved, but internally you are convinced that you don't deserve love? There are many reasons people think they don't deserve to be loved. Yet, there is no obstacle significant enough to prevent you from being loved by the right person for you. It is often our disregard for what we truly want and deserve in life that contributes to all the hurt and rejection we've experienced. Remember, you are worthy of love, no matter what happened in your past.

You Distrust the System

Have you ever been in a situation where you deserved to be trusted by someone and yet they doubted everything you did and questioned every statement you made? It is hurtful when this happens and such a relationship can't stand the test of time. The same rule applies to the system. You need to trust that it works in order for it to work in your favor. I've explained how everything in the universe is connected and works toward what is good, but if you don't trust the system, it won't deliver the results you desire. You need to become vulnerable in your trust and pure in your desires.

You Fear More Pain

People don't like to be vulnerable, as it is a position that leaves them open to feeling pain. Yet, being vulnerable is the bravest thing you can do. Brené Brown states that vulnerability is the only accurate way to measure courage (Jensen, 2019). You can't open your heart to love if you are not willing to make yourself vulnerable to the possibility that you might experience pain too. Yet, by doing so, you are being brave, and this strengthens the power of your desire and how you manifest love.

You Are Stuck in the Past

Let's be honest with each other here. Are you still hung up on an ex? Perhaps you are expressing your desire to find love, but what you truly desire is to reunite with an ex, and this desire is blocking you from receiving the love you deserve. If that relationship was meant to be, it would have lasted, but if not, forcing it will only put you on a path leading to more heartache and pain. Let go of your ex. The universe has something much greater in store for you, and you can't receive love with an open hand when you still have a clenched fist, holding on to something not worthy of who you are.

Employ Mindfulness or You'll Miss Vital Signs

Sometimes we ask for something, and are so intent on that thing coming into focus on the horizon, that we completely miss something better that was intended for us, passing us by. You need to be mindful and understand that what you receive might look a little different from what you've asked for, but it will always be better than imagined. Don't miss the signs.

Are You Sure You Seek Love?

A lesson I've learned the hard way is that we can deceive people, even ourselves, but not the universe. You can say that you want something and take all the steps to get what you want, but if that is not what you truly desire, you will get nothing. If you are not receiving the love you desire, question your intentions to see if that is what you truly want to manifest right now.

Manifesting Love Into Your Life

Are you ready to manifest being loved and loving the perfect partner for you? While you can use any of the many ways discussed this far to manifest your desires, including your desires for love, I've picked the following approach specifically for manifesting love. I think this is an especially helpful way to find what you seek in this regard.

- Reflect on your romantic past and the people who featured in it.
- You need to revert as far back as your first crush ever and, in chronological order, dissect each of these crushes or relationships.
- Expand on the following for each:

  ○ What was good about this relationship?
  ○ What was bad about it?
  ○ What is the worst memory you have of the time you had with this person?
  ○ What is the best thing that happened?

- When you have a comprehensive list of all the qualities and moments you didn't like, as well as the ones that made you happy, you have greater clarity on what you want to specify when stating your desire to the universe.
- Capture all the positive traits you want in this person.
- List all the aspects of a relationship you desire.

Be clear about not visualizing a specific person when you are writing these features, and also take care not to describe someone you already know and secretly want.

You just have to capture the features you desire and not give a description of someone you've already identified.

On the last page, you need to write down the things you'll do when you meet the right person. How do you want to improve yourself for this person?

- Do you want to lose weight?
- Should you stop sleeping with stuffed animals?
- Perhaps become neater in your surroundings?

You could even consider cleaning out a cupboard for the perfect person in your home.

Once you've identified these things, act on them straight away and make the improvement you would make for the perfect person. Usually, these are things you might be reluctant to do, and yet they leave you ashamed of yourself. Maybe you've had to hide certain aspects of who you are in previous relationships. Resolve these things and prepare yourself to receive the love you desire and deserve. This is how you remove any blockages, keeping you from the love of your life.

FINAL THOUGHTS

There are no limitations to what you want to manifest, and love is surely high on the list of things we all desire. Yet, you need to be clear on every aspect of what you want to manifest. Make sure your intentions are sincere, and identify and remove any obstacles that might keep you from enjoying the love and life you deserve.

6

MANIFESTING MONEY, SUCCESS, & MIRACLES

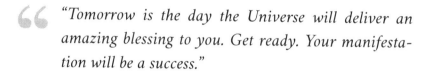

"Tomorrow is the day the Universe will deliver an amazing blessing to you. Get ready. Your manifestation will be a success."

— UNKNOWN

Success stories of manifestation that include money are so thrilling. Maybe it is because we all have this deep desire to enjoy financial freedom. In the advanced society we live in, finances are often the only thing that still have the power to keep us trapped in dead-end jobs.

The following success story is proof of how our limiting beliefs can cause the financial dilemmas we sometimes find ourselves in.

Sophie was the head of a medical practice, running it with three doctors and two full-time employees by her side. The practice was an immense success and generated fantastic profits. Yet, it also required long hours and, as Sophie was a mother, she wanted to spend more time with her children and less time at work.

She left the practice and opened a new practice with only her and a part-time assistant. The practice would only be open three days of the week, freeing up her time to spend with her children.

Soon, it became clear that this wasn't working. Running a practice is expensive, and they were not generating enough income. It was only once Sophie identified the beliefs holding her back that she could address this concern.

- Deep down, she was convinced that she wouldn't be able to do it on her own.
- She was sure that she needed more staff to make it work.
- Sophie was sure that to earn good money, you must work long hours.

The moment she addressed these beliefs and cleared them from her mind, her practice turned around. The very next month, the practice showed an amazing income of $30,000 (Castilla, 2021).

Sophie overcame the obstacles in her way and manifested her desire. What are the obstacles holding you back?

HOW CAN WE MANIFEST SUCCESS?

Let's jump right into some practical steps to help you manifest the financial status you desire.

Take Time for Deliberation

- What do you want?
- How do you define success?
- How will you know that you've successfully manifested this desire?

So often, people search for success, but do not know what success means to them. They'll say success is to be happy—

but happiness is not the same as success. It is a by-product of success, though, as you can also be happy without being financially successful.

Enjoying the successful manifestation of your financial desires would therefore require that you invest time before-hand to define what success means to you.

Take the time you need to consider your options before making any rushed decisions.

Establish your goals. The only way we can move forward in life is when we have clarity on which direction we are moving into. Thus, setting goals for yourself is a vital part of this journey. If you are unsure how to set goals effectively, I recommend you follow the SMART system to identify your goals. SMART goals are:

- **S**pecific
- **M**easurable
- **A**chievable
- **R**ealistic
- **T**imely

Next, you need to identify what excites you. The easiest way to make money and enjoy financial success is to earn an income from doing something you are passionate about. Identify what this is as part of your preparation.

MANIFESTING MONEY, SUCCESS, & MIRACLES | 127

Why do you want to enjoy financial success? Is your desire driven by greed alone or is there a noble cause for what you want to achieve? Also, make sure that you add a deadline to prevent procrastination and to maintain your momentum.

Once you have all the above in place, determine which goal you will work toward first. While it might feel like you are making faster progress by working on several goals at once, we only slow ourselves down when we spread ourselves too thin. Instead, take on one goal at a time.

Make Sure Your Mind Is Clear

Determine what the beliefs are that shape your life. Our beliefs are constantly being molded by our situation, life events, and a range of other factors. Sometimes our beliefs support us in our ventures, but it is also often the case that we hold on to limiting beliefs that don't serve us at all. Do a mental detox and get rid of every belief that doesn't contribute to your success.

Success Demands Complete Surrender

Doubt in the process places a break on your progress. To enjoy optimal success, you need to surrender yourself to the process of manifestation completely. There will be times when your mind will play tricks on you, but don't allow this to halt your progress, as you know that manifestation is more than magic. It is a proven concept with scientific evidence to back it up.

Stock Up on Positive Power

You know you need to be positive, but when you have no proof that things are going to work out, it is only human to feel disempowered, hopeless, desperate, trapped, and, of course, when you experience all these emotions, negativity takes over.

You can increase your positive vibes by:

- Keeping up with your gratitude journal.
- Spending time with positive people.
- Maintain your focus on what is good in your life.
- Know that every single day holds new opportunities, so don't let the negative experience of the previous day spill over.
- Use positive language when you speak.
- Identify the areas where you are predominantly negative and address them (Legg, 2019).

Allow Space for Imagination

Oh, I love daydreaming. It leaves me feeling all excited about what is possible and it inspires me to manifest these dreams that my creative mind developed for me to indulge in. Let your mind run free. Your mind is a safe space in which nothing can hold you down. Consider a life without mortgage payments, utility bills, and other responsibilities, giving you the freedom to build the life you desire without limitation. This is one way you can express your desires to the universe.

Remain in the Moment

The past is filled with regret, and the future may fill you with anxiety, but the present moment is free from any of this negativity. While your mind may continue to wander off in a different direction, always try to gently bring it back to the present moment.

Explore Your 'Why'

Why do you want to be successful? Why do you desire financial abundance? You need to know why you want all these things. If you don't, you might experience disappointment when you manifest your desires. It is also good to explore the reasons you want to manifest your success and wealth goals to be sure they are for the greater good.

Splurge on Gratitude and Be Generous

As I've mentioned several times, always make time for gratitude and show your appreciation for those things you are still waiting to receive. Generosity is also important. This generosity can involve your time or money. Maybe it even lies in skills or talents that you can share with someone without expecting something in return.

Be Open to Receiving

Make room in your life to accept the manifestation of your desires. If you want a lot of money, you need to be ready to receive a large sum. If you desire success, you must prepare your life and your circumstances to allow for this success. While you need to open yourself up in order to receive, you also need to prepare the foundation to fit this manifestation into your life.

THE MEANS TO MANIFEST

I believe that with manifesting specifically the wealth and success you desire, the following points all serve as means to assist you on this journey:

- Before you can manifest any wealth or success, you need to believe that wealth and prosperity are both a spiritual right you need to claim. They are yours, waiting for you to claim them.
- Always be open to exploring potential opportunities to generate money. Opportunities surround us, but we need to be mindful, otherwise we will miss them.

- Always replace negative thoughts by thinking about how your life will be when you have achieved the wealth you've set out to generate.
- Speak life into these desires. What type of energy are you projecting with your words? Remember, what you say will affect your future.
- Crush the doubt that lingers in your mind. Doubt is the nemesis of manifestation, and you won't be able to change your situation if you are not convinced that it will happen.
- Stop fearing wealth. Often we want more money, but deep inside we consider money and wealth evil. We use a range of negative terms when we describe wealthy people. If this is the case for you, you are sending mixed signals into the universe and slowing down your progress.
- Stay committed until you see results. The problem with quitting is that you never know how far you are from success. Maybe you only needed to persist for another day, week, or month, and your entire situation could have made a turnaround. So, please don't quit until you see results (Ghabani, 2021).

10 STEPS TO MANIFEST MONEY

Would you like to have a 10-step program to follow in order to help you manifest wealth and success?

Here you go:

- **Step 1:** Know what you want to do with the money you want to manifest. Would you like to purchase property, travel the world, pay for your kids' education, or maybe just live without financial stress? Write down your reasons.
- **Step 2:** How much would you need to make this happen? You need to determine how much money would mean financial freedom to you. Create a

spreadsheet of how much money you would need and write that number down.

- **Step 3:** Shed all your limiting beliefs. We've covered how limiting beliefs hold you back and even learned how Sophie turned around the financial situation of her clinic when she shattered her limiting beliefs.
- **Step 4:** Pretend you are wealthy until you are. When you are poor, you have the mindset of a poor person and thus you attract more of the same energy. When you pretend to be rich, this is the energy you send into the universe, and it will reflect back to you.
- **Step 5:** Transform your beliefs. Reprogram your mind from claiming that money is bad and turns people to evil, to enjoying having money and the freedom it brings.
- **Step 6:** Just like a vision board, you can also create a dream board for your financial desires. This board can contain images of money and pictures of things that symbolize wealth and financial independence to you.
- **Step 7:** Visualization is good, but offering greater detail is even better. The more detail you add to your visualizations, the harder it becomes for the mind to distinguish between what is real and what is not. It is how you open yourself up to receive wealth.
- **Step 8:** Become familiar with the smell of money. Does the idea of sniffing money make you giggle?

This is okay. However, smell is one of your senses, and the more you become familiar with money by using all your senses, the better your visualizations will be.

- **Step 9:** How would having money change your life? What would it mean to you on a personal level to have money? How will your style of dress, your home, and your lifestyle change when you are wealthy? Explore these changes and teach yourself what it would be like to be rich.
- **Step 10:** You might not have a lot yet, but you need to be grateful for what you have. If you can't express gratitude for what you have or what you are bound to receive, your manifestations might just not happen (Hurst, 2015).

MORE TIPS TO MANIFEST MONEY

While you are busy working through the 10 steps above, you can also bulk up your efforts by following these tips on how to increase your wealth:

Explore Money Rituals

What are your money rituals? Maybe you aren't even aware of the fact that you follow certain rituals with your money. Examples of these rituals would be checking your bank balance daily, and keeping a spreadsheet to have a record of your income and expenses. Another ritual can be to set financial goals for yourself. By following these rituals, you are improving your relationship with money and learning how to use it to your advantage.

Get a Money Spell Jar

Some people like to have what they call a "money spell jar." Manifestation has nothing to do with magic, but if you want to increase the positivity of your vibration for finances, a bit of magic may just be the excitement you are looking for. Get a jar and on it, write down all the things you want to do with your money. Keep the notes in your spell jar and see how you manifest abundance.

Use Money Manifestation Rituals

Just like how you can use affirmations, you can also create money manifestation rituals. These are nothing but positive affirmations regarding your financial position. In the same manner as affirmations, you need to say these lines to yourself out loud. Examples of these lines would be:

- I attract wealth and abundance into my life.
- I deserve to be financially free.
- I am qualified to receive what I desire.

Meditation on Money

Ever heard of money meditation? The core of meditation is to focus your mind on one thought alone. Why not make money the one idea and have it in abundance?

Closely linked to meditation would be money mantras. What would your money mantra be? Are you willing to send this desire into the universe?

Start a Money Manifestation Journal

A money manifestation journal would strengthen the desires you reflect in the universe and help you keep track of the progress you are making.

Fake It

Then finally, fake it till you make it. Yes, I am advising this again. As long as you fake something, you are pretending as if what you desire is already present in your life. This way, you immerse yourself in positive energy that will attract more of the same (Holly, 2022).

EXAMPLES OF MONEY MANTRAS AND AFFIRMATIONS

For some inspiration, you can look at these effective money mantras:

- I choose to be financially free.
- I am worthy of success and financial abundance.
- I naturally attract wealth and success.
- Money flows freely in my direction.

THE THREE-DAY MONEY MANIFESTATION MIRACLE

While it is unnecessary to control the time of manifestations, as they will happen when they have to happen, it is also good to know that we can realize our desires in as little as three days. When I say desires, it can be something as vast as getting a million dollars unexpectedly.

The three-day miracle is based on the work of Neville Goddard. I urge you to explore more of his work, as Goddard was a pioneer in manifestation. I want to share something quite impactful that he himself shared with the world: It is the belief that if you go through life, believing you are already the person you want to be or already have what you want to manifest in your life, and you do so without a doubt, then it will manifest in your life within only three days (Neyah, n.d.).

How would this look in reality? If you simply desire to have a certain amount of money, your desire is pure and for the greater good, you write down your desires, talk about them as if you've already received them, and are grateful for what you have—then you will receive it within three days.

Are you still feeling skeptical about it? Of course, you can have your doubts. However, what I want to ask you is this: What do you have to lose? Why would you not want to try something and throw yourself fully into the concept if you can only gain from it? Wouldn't that be sinking your opportunity to enjoy greatness in life before you've even given it a fair chance?

THE 369 METHOD

More success stories for manifesting money refer to using the 369 Method. One such success story comes from Andy Lawson, who manifested $90,000 in only three days.

Lawson explains how he wanted to manifest $80,000 quite simply: He wrote down his aspirations as if they were already his reality. He emphasizes that you need to be extremely specific about what you desire and add as much detail to it as you can.

More specifically, he wrote down his goals three times in the morning, six times during the afternoon, and nine times before he went to bed. For three days, he did this diligently. He planned to manifest this goal in 30 days, as that is the usual timeline he set for himself to manifest any desire in his life. Yet, when he employed this method, it took only three days until he received a phone call stating investors were keen to invest $90,000 in his coaching services. He immediately jumped at the opportunity and was set. While this desire took only three days to manifest, he also got more than what he asked for (Lawson, n.d.).

MANIFESTING MONEY IN YOUR LIFE

Several exercises will help you manifest the wealth and abundance you seek in your life. I want to walk you through one of these exercises to set you on the road to success.

The exercise is called "Spend a Million Dollars." Sounds like fun, right? You will need to remain committed to the process for 30 days, and during this time, you are reprogramming your brain to make positive connections with money and, even more importantly, spending money. You can start a new journal for the process or use your money manifestation journal.

Step 1: Visualize that you have $1,000 to spend any way you wish. What would you purchase? Record how you feel when you purchase the product. Why did you choose that item and what emotions did you experience when you made the purchase? You can describe the product in detail and even stick an image of the item in your journal. On the second day, you will do the same exercise, but this time you have $2,000 to spend.

Step 2: Continue with this process and increase your daily expense to $10,000 on day 10.

Step 3: From day 11 onwards, you increase your daily spending by $10,000 per day until you get to $100,000 on day 20.

Step 4: From day 21 to the end of the month, you increase your daily budget by $100,000 until you get to $1 million.

This is how you gradually change your mindset regarding money and free yourself from the internal friction holding you from your riches (Manifesting Money Exercises, 2021).

FINAL THOUGHTS

I am going to make a wild statement. I think when we compare the desire to manifest love and the desire to manifest success and wealth, we'll see that far more people dream about money. You have all the steps and tips to manifest the financial situation you desire. Why not start right now to manifest the financial position you want to be in?

In the next chapter, I will walk you through several more techniques you can employ to manifest anything you desire.

7

THE BEST TECHNIQUES TO ATTRACT EVERYTHING YOU WANT

66 *"To the mind that is still, the whole universe surrenders."*

— LAO TZU

Up to this point, we've covered several manifestation techniques, which were very specific to certain types of manifestation you might want in your life. However, there are many more techniques, and in this chapter, I am going to summarize some of the most effective and widely employed techniques.

THE GRATITUDE STACKING METHOD

This is most likely the simplest method to follow to manifest your desires. It comprises only three easy steps.

Jot down every person, object, or situation you are grateful for.

Once you are done, take your time and read through everything you've listed. Say it out loud to yourself, and recall a memory related to a specific point you are grateful for.

Spend about 20 seconds to a minute allowing the sense of gratitude you feel for each of these things to flow through you. While the method mentions a time frame, I want to urge you to take as much time as you need. Just don't rush through the items.

Add to this list every day. Some days you might have more time and can add 10 or more entries, while other days you might be more rushed and only have time for three. As you progress, you are creating a very extensive list, capturing all you are grateful for in your life.

Keep in mind that you should always write in the present tense, even if what you are expressing gratitude for has yet to come (Manifestation: The Stacking Method, n.d.).

Your sentences would most likely start in the following manner:

- I am so grateful for...
- Thank you for...
- I am so happy about...

THE TIME-LAPSE METHOD

The method also depends on a foundation of gratitude. You will list an equal number of items you are grateful for from the past, present, and future. However, once you've compiled the list, you need to scramble the items so that the future item can be found at any position on your list.

For example, the order may be: you are grateful for meeting your partner two years ago, for the way your co-worker helped you out today, and for the promotion you are going to have in the future. As you write these in the present tense, though, you eliminate the time frame in your life. So, when you read through your list and spend 20 or more seconds on every item, it will appear as:

- I am grateful for my promotion to advance my career and increase my income.
- I am grateful for my partner, who loves me deeply and whom I love.
- I am grateful for the support from my coworkers.

The techniques work exceptionally well for people who make major changes to their lives, as it reduces the stress and struggles often accompanying these changes. It is easy and fun, and works wonders for improving your vibration to attract things you desire, but haven't received yet.

What happens in your life when you use this technique is that your beliefs gradually just adjust to the desires you have with no effort. The technique is also known to increase confidence (The Time-Lapse Method in Manifestation, 2021).

THE GRATITUDE BLITZING METHOD

This method requires that you look around at your surroundings and list the things you are grateful for as part of the Room Blitz. Next, you think about the people in your life and why you are grateful for each of them as part of the People Blitz, and lastly, as part of the Moment Blitz, consider all the moments in your life that you appreciate for how they've contributed to shaping you into the person you are.

You can opt to do all three of the Blitz exercises, vary between them, or pick one version for the day. It is a simple exercise, and you'll have so much fun while doing it and raising your vibration to a state of happiness.

An added feature to this exercise, which you can choose to use if you feel like it, is to expand on every point you list by stating why you are grateful for this object, person, or experience in your life. Once you are done making your list, say the words "thank you" out loud. Be sure to say it with sincere emotions and as many times as you feel like (The Blitz Method in Manifestation, 2021).

THE DISCOUNT TRIGGER METHOD

I want to share the story behind this method, since I believe it will help you to truly understand how it works and because I find it so endearing.

An entrepreneur started his business, but soon after opening his doors, clients returned a faulty item he was selling. The product cost $50, and many customers wanted a full refund. Needless to say, this ate into his profits right away.

To save his business, he promoted a product selling at $300, but he would give all the customers who were unhappy with the $50 item a $100 discount, as he felt bad about what happened. This gesture of goodwill worked in his favor, and many of the customers who asked for a refund on the first item now supported him. Through these customers, he made far more profit than from customers who didn't complain. He turned what happened into his business strategy, and every time someone asked for a refund, he would give them a discount on a more expensive item in his store, and his business flourished.

This method teaches us that when bad things happen, you can have a positive response in place. Say you are in a rush to get to work, and when you want to start your car, the battery is dead. You can either grind your teeth and be upset about being late, or you can use the moment to be grateful that you have a car, and that it is only the battery that is faulty. When your manager is finding fault with everything you do, you can decide to get negative and despondent about your career, or you can use this for a moment of gratitude for the signal that you can find a better position.

The method helps you to use a trigger of negative energy in order to boost your positive vibrations (The Discount Trigger Method in Manifestation, 2021).

THE PENNIES TO MILLIONS METHOD

Which task seems less likely to happen, finding a penny a day or finding $100,000? I am sure most would say that the likelihood of finding a penny is far higher. I mean, most people have picked up money in an unexpected place at some point in their lives. Yet, what we forget is that the universe doesn't see small amounts of money or large numbers. No, it just sees money, and it will always keep a consistent flow of money aimed in your direction.

Thus, ask for a penny a day and you will most likely find that or even more. Be open to receiving this flow of money into your life. Regardless of whether it is a small or a large amount, you will always be reminded that the flow exists and you need to be open to receive it. I am not saying that you need to keep your head down now in a constant search for money, but be mindful that it will happen (The Pennies to Millions Method to Manifest Financial Abundance, 2021).

One example where this happened for me was when I asked for a penny, and by late afternoon, I had received nothing yet. I geared up for my normal jog in the park, and as I came to the last stretch, a $5 bill blew right across my path. I received 500 times what I asked. Always express gratitude when this happens.

THE STORY SCRIPTING METHOD

If you had to recall one day from your past, whether yester-day, a day about a year ago, or even a day from your child-hood, it would be easy. You can capture the details of the day and how events on that day made you feel.

Scripting your future can also be easy. You can start every day by scripting the day ahead and pretending you already live the life you desire.

Start this story with a statement of gratitude. What are you grateful for on the day you are scripting? Explain why you are grateful for this in your life. Then, you can proceed to write as much as you like about the day you are looking forward to from the perspective of already living the life you desire. Don't write less than one page, but you can continue to write as much as you like.

Once you are done, give thanks, as you know that what you want to manifest already exists and will enter your reality soon. Through this method, you instruct both the universe and the law of attraction on how to receive what you desire (The Story Scripting Method in Manifestation, 2021).

THE STATEMENT SCRIPTING METHOD

In the previous method, you would script your entire story of the day. In this method, you would zoom in on one thing you desire and want to manifest in your life. Identify the one desire you want to manifest and pick one specific statement to confirm this desire. Rewrite that statement repeatedly on a piece of paper at least 15 times, or more if you desire.

While doing this, notice the way it makes you feel, knowing that what you desire already exists. Don't just half-heartedly write the same line over and over again. You need to be convinced that your desire has been created for you, that it is yours, and that it is bound to enter your life soon. Claim this as your manifestation.

At the end of your session, always give thanks for this manifestation, as gratitude is very magnetic and attracts all you like into your life (The Statement Scripting Method in Manifestation, 2021).

THE WALKING MEDITATION METHOD

Writing down the desires you want to manifest is a powerful way of achieving what you want, but there may be times when you want to do something else. Why not try the walking meditation method?

Decide what location allows you to feel comfortable. It should be a place where you can move around and feel safe, without distractions.

Start walking. Take 10 or 20 steps forward. Take these steps slowly and deliberately and develop a rhythm throughout. At the end of your steps, stop and turn around, and then walk back in the same manner.

Be aware of your legs, the feeling of your feet on the ground, and how you lift them to take the next step on your way. Pay attention to the sounds, the sensations you feel, and if you smell anything.

Focus on the desires you want to manifest and what your spiritual needs are. Whenever your mind drifts off, gently bring it back to your center and reclaim your focus.

Through this form of meditation, you employ your entire being to focus on just the one thought—namely, what you desire. Use this method to strengthen the connection between mind, body, and soul (Kabat-Zinn, 2022).

FINAL THOUGHTS

For manifestation and using universal laws, you have several options to choose from. The ones I shared here are the most widely used, and this will give you a good foundation with which to start your journey. I recommend that you experiment with several of these methods to see which one suits you best in terms of manifesting your desires. Which method will you try first?

8

LAW OF ASSUMPTION

66 *"Dare to believe in the reality of your assumption and watch the world play its part relative to its fulfillment."*

— NEVILLE GODDARD

The law of assumption is one of the 12 universal laws, and I wanted to end this book by shifting the focus to assumption, and how you can use it to manifest your desires.

WHAT IS THE LAW OF ASSUMPTION?

Manifestation wouldn't be possible without the law of assumption. By means of this law, we assume what we want already exists, and that we only need to receive it. It is how we can manifest things into our reality and change our lives to what we want them to be like.

The law enables us to consider what we want, be specific about it, and believe that we have it. It allows us to change our behavior and be open to receiving what we want to manifest.

I also just want to remind you here that while the two are closely interdependent, it is not the same as the law of attraction. Through the law of attraction, you can attract your desires, while the law of assumption allows you to assume your desire is already part of your life.

HOW DOES THE LAW OF ASSUMPTION WORK?

For this explanation, I am reverting to the work of Neville Goddard, as he did exceptional work exploring the wonder and workings of manifestation.

Goddard stated that within the human mind, there is a oneness with God, and that the world we are living in and perceive as our reality is merely a physical manifestation of what is taking place in the consciousness. What this means is that the physical world, which many perceive as reality, is determined by a person's experiences and beliefs. If your conscious mind is predominantly negative, you will live in a reality that is not pleasant nor favorable. The same goes when you are more positive and operate on high vibrations. What this effectively means is that you can change your reality by changing your mindset, as you assume what is taking place in your mind is real.

Two key points I need to highlight regarding this law are the following:

First, you need to assume that what you desire is already created for you and you already have it. If you believe you are reaching for this, you will remain in a state of reaching, but never possessing. So, please don't assume that you will get it, or that it is bound to happen, or that you are going to do something, for then you will be stuck in this state. You must assume it is already yours, that you did in fact receive it, or that you did do it. Remain in the present and don't refer to the future.

The second point is that you need to persist in maintaining a state of mind affirming you've already received what you desire. This needs to become your constant state, your inner reality, and what you believe every moment of every day. To sustain this belief and help you persist through it all, you can use a journal or affirmations.

INCORPORATING THE LAW OF ASSUMPTION INTO YOUR LIFE

You can employ the law of assumption to manifest your desires in any area of your life, but let's focus on the following common areas for desired change:

Personal Success

Success symbolizes something different for everyone. For you, does success represent a new career, a promotion, or perhaps the house or car of your dreams? You can employ this law by assuming that you've already received what you desire. Assume that what you are dreaming about is already yours and present in your life (Manasa, 2021).

Romance

Maybe your biggest desire is to find the right partner, who would love you unconditionally. Do you realize that this particular person is already out there? That it is only a matter of time until the right circumstances unfold and bring you two together? The law of assumption states that you need to assume this is the case and by doing so, you can change your outlook on romance as if that person is already in your life (Manasa, 2021).

Optimal Health and Fitness

Goddard stated that the physical world we know is created by our minds, so we can impact our physical appearance through the law of assumption too. Yes, living a healthy and balanced life requires discipline, but it doesn't all have to take sweat and effort. Adopt the mindset of already being healthy and fit, sustaining the body you desire. Find the level of fitness and the appearance you desire through a collaboration of physical effort and making the necessary mind shift (Manasa, 2021).

Improve Who You Are

Do you sometimes wish you were more patient, driven, kind, compassionate, or any other attribute you appreciate in others? How will this change your life, relationships, and perspectives? How will it improve your state of happiness? Assume that you are already that person—behave like you would behave as that person, and see how your life transforms (Manasa, 2021).

Increase Your Wealth

Do you want to be rich? How large does your bank account need to be for you to feel that way? What assets do you need to own for that to happen? You can remove the mental blocks keeping you from enjoying this life by assuming you are already enjoying this wealth. This is how you break the limiting patterns in your life, holding you from what has been created especially for you (Manasa, 2021).

The Law of Assumption and Manifestation

The universal law states that nothing exists if it is not part of your consciousness. Based on this, we can say that if you want something to be part of your reality, then you can transform your reality by changing what is taking place in your mind. You can shape your life and manifest your desires by assuming you already have what you desire, and this way, it manifests into reality.

Act as if you've already achieved what you desire and visualize a vivid experience of what life would be like, and what it would feel like, when your desires are a reality.

STEPS TO FOLLOW FOR THE LAW OF ASSUMPTION

Sometimes people find Goddard's explanation challenging to grasp. This is especially the case when you are new to manifestation. While I would always urge others to expand on their knowledge regarding every aspect of manifestation and how the 12 universal laws impact our lives, I don't want anyone to get bogged down in the details. True inspiration and motivation are nestled in seeing the results you desire manifested in your life.

Therefore, using the law of assumption is an easy entry point when you are keen on exploring how you can transform your life through manifestation, as you only need to follow three easy steps for this exercise. These are:

Step 1: Capture Your Desires in Writing

Again, the manifestation depends largely on the power of the written word. As this is coupled with sharing your desires with clarity, it would serve you well to write down what it is you desire. Start by only focusing on one thing. Expand on how manifesting this desire makes you feel, what you see differently in your life, and what senses this manifestation triggers.

Step 2: Immerse Yourself in the Emotions

When you assume that your dreams have been manifested, you will sense a surge of positive emotions. So, instead of just writing about your desires and what life is like when they are part of your reality, take a moment to feel every emotion. Allow the desires you are manifesting to change your internal state.

Step 3: Assume Your Desire Is Fulfilled

Get up and approach life with the assumption that the desires you've expressed have already been fulfilled and are part of your life. Do the things you would do when this is your reality. Furthermore, think the kind of thoughts this new reality is stirring, feel the emotions, identify the goals you want to achieve, and live life as someone who already has everything you want, for this is what assumption allows you to do.

By opting to approach life as if you've already received everything you want, you program your subconscious mind to create a life that represents your assumptions in reality by influencing your actions and thoughts.

The beauty of the law of assumption is that it works every time (Wong, 2021).

HOW TO SPEED UP THE PROCESS

While I am a firm believer that manifestation takes place in a time and manner that may differ from what we expect, there are ways in which you can speed up the process. I think this can be especially helpful during the early days, when you are manifesting for the first time in your life.

I am sharing these steps to help you grow your confidence in the process and so that you can shape the life you desire.

Before I jump right into these steps, I want to remind you that the law of assumption is what many would refer to as the key ingredient of manifestation. What is even more interesting is that you are already applying this law to everything you do. Throughout your life, every single day, there are things you assume will happen in a certain manner, and as you assumed it would happen, it happens. Often, though, we expect the worst; we assume our fears will become our reality. We assume that life will be hard and that we will only enjoy great wealth if we work extremely hard for long hours. We assume we will be disappointed, fail, and struggle, and guess what? We are disappointed, we fail, and we struggle. And these challenges only strengthen our beliefs that life is challenging.

How will your life look different if you take on every challenge with the assumption that it will work out well, that others will agree with your opinion, and that you can make a lot of money even when you are working much shorter hours?

Why are we so keen to manifest negativity in our lives and not the opposite? Whether there is an accurate answer to this question, I can't say. What is important, though, is that we understand how important the law of assumption is when we are manifesting our desires.

Another point I want to emphasize is that we are not even aware of the many assumptions shaping our lives. These assumptions develop in our subconscious mind, and when you take control of your subconscious mind, you can change the assumptions you have, along with the reality you shape for yourself to live in.

How easy or hard is that?

The first step is to identify any limiting beliefs blocking your mind. As long as your beliefs are limiting you, it will be impossible to manifest your desires. Your limiting beliefs will keep you from assuming anything that is not aligned with them. What I am essentially saying is that you can get anything you want, as long as you first clear your existing negative beliefs and replace them with positive beliefs, so you can have positive assumptions to shape your reality with.

The challenge most people struggle with is that they are unaware of the assumptions they have, they accept the state of their lives as all there is for them in this world, and they take their struggles as evidence, confirming their mindset.

We also have many other assumptions that we don't even consider. You assume that you'll wake up the next morning, that your car will be where you left it, that it will start when you turn the key in the ignition, that you will find the food you need when you go to the grocery store, and the list goes on. Sometimes, certain events take place wherein, on these rare occasions, what you've assumed didn't happen. Maybe you turn the key and your car battery is flat; you go to the grocery store and the specific item you are looking for is out of stock. But these occasions are outliers and not the norm.

Let's use this in our favor.

First, you need to determine how much you truly believe that you already have what you want. This is important, as you need to believe good will come and that you have the power to manifest your desires as much as you've been manifesting your obstacles.

Close your eyes and say to yourself, "I have," and then complete the sentence with what you desire. Likewise, consider saying "I am," and complete the sentence with what you want to be. Think this not only in your head, but say it out loud too. Say it in the same manner as you would make any other statement about your current situation. For example, just as you would tell a friend you are struggling to find clients, tell yourself so much work is flowing into your business in abundance. Did it feel weird or did it feel normal? If it felt the same as making any other statement, then you have dealt with your limiting beliefs. If it felt weird and as if you had to force yourself to get the words out, then there are still beliefs blocking you from shaping your reality.

In the latter case, you need to go back to the drawing board and truly clear out your mind of any limiting beliefs.

You know your beliefs are true, sincere, and strong when you react with shock when anyone suggests the opposite of what you are believing. When this happens, you know that you have overcome the limitations of your programming up to this point in your life. It is the programming that most people have, enabling them to believe that their current circumstances prove their reality, while they remain unaware of their contribution to their finances, love, happiness, and success.

For you to manifest anything in life, you need to believe that it is possible without a shred of doubt, and the only way to overcome doubt is to work through your limiting beliefs and resolve them. By doing so, you can speed up the process of manifestation by using the law of assumption in your favor (Kate, n.d.).

FINAL THOUGHTS

Being able to manifest your desires to shape the life you've always wanted is only possible when you've mastered the law of assumption. While thinking about the law of assumption might be a new concept to you, you've been practicing it all your life. Have you ever gone to bed and not assumed that you'd wake up the next day? We are so used to assuming certain things that we don't even realize that we are doing it. It is like breathing. You don't count the number of breaths you take every day. You don't even think about the fact that you are breathing, and yet your life depends on it.

In the same way, you don't think about all the assumptions you make, or how they shape your reality, yet every second of your day is determined by assumptions.

All you need to do now is change your approach to assumptions and no longer be disempowered by them. This can be achieved by not allowing your subconscious to control those assumptions, while simultaneously letting your conscious mind clear any obstacle to creating the life you want by using assumptions that serve you.

CONCLUSION

What would it take for you to believe that manifestation works? Would it be easier if I told you that manifestation is a new concept driven by advances in technology and now you have the power to transform your life? I hope not, for what I've told you is that you've always had the power to control your life, and there is nothing new about manifestation. It is an age-old technique trusted for generations, employed by many, and forgotten by an even larger group of people.

While technology and modern advancements can be highly beneficial to help us create the lives we desire and to manifest our dreams, they will never be nearly as effective as exploring, discovering, and employing the ancient laws and practices covered in this book.

Manifestation might sound like magic, like a story about make-believe practices, and many even consider it to be evil. But what those people don't realize is while they are championing against manifestation, they live their lives guided by assumptions and manifestation.

It is almost as if it is easier to assume and believe negative outcomes will become our reality than to follow the same practice centered on positive beliefs.

You know better now. In this book, I've provided you with enough scientific facts to have a solid foundation for further exploration. I have shared numerous exercises to enable you to put every statement I've made to the test.

I've provided you with explanations and shared additional resources to further quench your search for wisdom, as I support continuous growth and would like for you to learn more about everything there is to learn.

We've even discovered what the reason could be, if you are not enjoying the success you desire, and how to address those obstacles.

Now, I want you to define your desires and to state with absolute clarity and conviction to the universe how you want your reality to look. Believe that whatever your desire is, it has already been created just for you, and all that is left for you to do is to receive it with gratitude.

Manifestation works wonders! But to make it work, you must believe in yourself and the universe, and that everything you wish for will come true—as long as you align yourself with it. It's time to take a leap and start attracting the things that your heart desires.

If you've enjoyed this enriching experience, please invite others to share in the knowledge, too, by giving me a positive review.

During the past 12 years, I've been able to create the exact life I desired. I've been able to shape my reality. Not because I have any special powers or enjoyed any privileges, but because I was introduced to the power of manifestation at an early stage. This allowed me to shape my entire belief system around what is possible and out there, waiting for me. It enabled me to live with the belief that I have received everything good, wholesome, or prosperous, and all is intended for me.

It boils down to one decision: Are you ready to choose life?

REFERENCES

6 Signs you aren't in alignment. (2022, March 2). Ellduclos. https://www.ellduclos.blog/signs-you-arent-in-alignment-soul-purpose/

6 Ways to practice fitness for the soul. (n.d.). Plum Deluxe. https://www.plumdeluxe.com/fitness-for-the-soul

10 Powerful manifestation techniques to help you succeed. (n.d.). https://www.abundancenolimits.com/10-powerful-manifestation-techniques/

A quote by Gautama Buddha. (n.d.). Goodreads. https://www.goodreads.com/quotes/1296640-all-that-we-are-is-the-result-of-what-we

A quote from A Return to Love. (n.d.). Goodreads. https://www.goodreads.com/quotes/928-our-deepest-fear-is-not-that-we-are-inadequate-our

A quote from so you want to be a wizard. (n.d.). Goodreads. https://www.goodreads.com/quotes/525709-believe-something-and-the-universe-is-on-its-way-to

Amit Ray quote. (n.d.). Lib Quotes. https://libquotes.com/amit-ray/quote/lba7x9s

The Blitz Method in Manifestation. (2021, October 1). High Income Source. https://highincomesource.com/the-blitz-method-in-manifestation/

Brown, J., & Wong, J. (2017, June 6). *How gratitude changes you and your brain.* Greater Good. https://greatergood.berkeley.edu/article/item/how_gratitude_changes_you_and_your_brain

Buzzell, A. (2021, February 9). *How to manifest love into your life using the law of attraction, according to an expert.* PureWow. https://www.purewow.com/wellness/how-to-manifest-love

Byrne, R. (2016). *The secret : the 10th anniversary edition.* Atria Books ; Hillsboro, Or.

Carpenter, D. (2018). *The science behind gratitude (and how it can change your life).* Happify. https://www.happify.com/hd/the-science-behind-gratitude/

Castilla, M. (2021, June 23). *Manifesting money success stories - using law of attraction effectively.* Miriam Castilla | Manifesting Abundance. https://miriamcastilla.com/107-manifesting-money-success-stories/

CFI Team. (2022, May 7). *SMART Goal - Definition, guide, and importance of goal setting.* Corporate Finance Institute. https://corporatefinanceinstitute.com/resources/knowledge/other/smart-goal/

Chupinina·, V. (2021, August 2). *Why the law of assumption is the best for manifesting.* Amodrn. https://amodrn.com/law-of-assumption/

Clark, J. (n.d.). *Manifestation exercise #27 – Attracting the perfect love partner or relationship.* Law of Attraction and Resource Guide. https://www.lawofattractionresourceguide.com/manifestation-exercise-27-attracting-the-perfect-love-partner-or-relationship/

Deane, S. (2018, October 9). *Ways to improve your mind, body and soul.* Park Regency Thornton. https://www.parkregencythornton.com/blog/ways-to-improve-your-mind-body-and-soul

The Discount Trigger Method in Manifestation. (2021, October 1). High Income Source. https://highincomesource.com/the-discount-trigger-method-in-manifestation/

Esther. (2020, June 7). *11 Common law of attraction mistakes that stop you manifesting.* Through the Phases. https://www.throughthephases.com/law-of-attraction-mistakes/

The Fox. (n.d.). *20 Law of attraction exercises to practise daily.* Thriveglobal.com. https://thriveglobal.com/stories/20-law-of-attraction-exercises-to-practise-daily/

Getting into spiritual alignment. (n.d.). Soul Success Unleashed. https://soulsuccessunleashed.com/spiritual-awakening/spiritual-alignment/

Ghabani, B. (2021, September 27). *8 Keys to manifesting money.* Linkedin. https://www.linkedin.com/pulse/8-keys-manifesting-money-boulefaa-ghabani/

Girlboss. (2022, January 1). *20 Money mantras to inspire financial freedom.* Girlboss. https://girlboss.com/blogs/read/money-mantras-affirmations

Hall, A. C. (n.d.). *8 Steps to connect with the universe and create the life you want.* Thriveglobal. https://thriveglobal.com/stories/8-steps-to-connect-with-the-universe-and-create-the-life-you-want/

Holly. (2022, February 17). *How to manifest money — 10 Money manifestation tips that actually work.* Holly Habeck. https://hollyhabeck.com/2022/02/17/how-to-manifest-money-manifestation/

Houlis, A. (2021, November 11). *3 Legitimate ways to manifest the kind of love you deserve.* Shape. https://www.shape.com/lifestyle/sex-and-love/how-to-manifest-love

Hurst, K. (2014, May 30). *Simple 10 minute manifestation exercises.* The Law of Attraction. https://thelawofattraction.com/simple-10-minute-manifestation-exercises/

Hurst, K. (2015, November 26). *Is it possible to manifest money? 10 Steps manifesting money.* The Law of Attraction. https://thelawofattraction.com/really-possible-manifest-money/

Hurst, K. (2017, August 4). *How to manifest love with a specific person.* The Law of Attraction. https://thelawofattraction.com/how-to-manifest-love/

Jensen, E. (2019, April 19). *5 takeaways on vulnerability from Brené Brown's "The Call To Courage."* USA TODAY. https://www.usatoday.com/story/life/tv/2019/04/19/brene-brown-call-courage-netflix-vulnerability/3497969002/

Kabat-Zinn, J. (2022, February 24). *Walking meditation guide: How to meditate while walking.* Masterclass Articles. https://www.masterclass.com/articles/walking-meditation-guide#4-benefits-of-walking-meditation

Kabić, J. (2021, August 15). *How to manifest love [What you should do to find love].* Review42. https://review42.com/resources/how-to-manifest-love/

Kate, M. (n.d.). *Manifest using the law of assumption.* Www.youtube.com. https://www.youtube.com/watch?v=6BZVsUbGO-8

Kate, M. (n.d.). *The ultimate law of attraction hack.* Www.youtube.com. https://www.youtube.com/watch?v=QTJnRbFJvvE&t=1s

Kate, M. (n.d.). *You'll never look at manifestation the same again...* Youtube. https://www.youtube.com/watch?v=2KsgO6zlRQ0

Kimmel, S. (2016, August 26). *Food for the soul.* Live Your Life. https://www.liveyourlifept.com/blog/2016/08/26/food-for-the-soul/

Lao Tzu Quotes. (n.d.). BrainyQuote. https://www.brainyquote.com/quotes/lao_tzu_133381

Lawson, A. (n.d.). *How I manifested $90,000 in 3 days.* Journal. https://vocal.media/journal/how-i-manifested-90-000-in-3-days

Legg, T. J. (2019, February 21). *How to think positive and have an optimistic outlook: 8 Tips.* Healthline. https://www.healthline.com/health/how-to-think-positive#tips

LOA Admin. (2022, February 13). *Law of attraction statistics, trends and scientific facts 2022.* DreamMaker. https://dreammaker.co.uk/law-of-attraction/facts-stats/

Ludwig, S. (2021, May 16). *Start a spiritual journal.* Canyon Ranch. https://www.canyonranch.com/well-stated/post/start-a-spiritual-journal/

Maatta, P. (2021, February 16). *9 Ways to practice the law of attraction daily.* The Law of Attraction Blog by DreamMaker. https://dreammaker.co.uk/blog/how-do-you-practice-law-of-attraction/

Manasa. (2021, November 14). *Law Of Assumption: Neville Goddard's magical formula of life.* Wealthfulmind.com. https://wealthfulmind.com/law-of-assumption-neville-goddard-formula/

Manifestation | How to manifest desires. (2022, April 27). The Official Website of the Secret. https://www.thesecret.tv/manifestation/

Manifestation: The Stacking Method. (n.d.). High Income Source. https://highincomesource.com/manifestation-the-stacking-method/

Manifesting money exercises. (2021, September 26). High Income Source. https://highincomesource.com/manifesting-money-exercises/

Master the law of attraction and create abundance with Rhonda Byrne. (2020, November 25). Lewis Howes. https://lewishowes.com/podcast/master-the-law-of-attraction-create-abundance-using-your-mind-with-the-secret-creator-rhonda-byrne/

Matejko, S. (2019, July 10). *Spiritual alignment: 11 things to say when you're out of alignment.* I AM & CO. https://iamandco.com/blogs/articles/spiritual-alignment

Maya Angelou Quote. (n.d.). A-Z Quotes. https://www.azquotes.com/quote/344894

Mayo Clinic. (2022, April 29). *A beginner's guide to meditation.* Mayo Clinic. https://www.mayoclinic.org/tests-procedures/meditation/in-depth/meditation/art-20045858

Money affirmations that will attract money, wealth and abundance. (2020, January 14). Mom Money Map. https://mommoneymap.com/money-affirmations/

Neimark, J. (2012, June 19). *Sleep: What you need to know.* Spirituality & Health. https://www.spiritualityhealth.com/articles/2012/06/19/sleep-what-you-need-know

NEVILLE GODDARD quotes about "Assumption". (n.d.). Inspiring Quotes.

https://www.inspiringquotes.us/author/5700-neville-goddard/about-assumption

Neyah. (n.d.). *Manifest anything that you want in less than three days Neville law of assumption.* Www.youtube.com. https://www.youtube.com/watch?v=bym9dx0azRA

O'Connell, E. (2022, February 5). *Believe it, achieve it: Five manifestation success stories.* Metro. https://metro.co.uk/2022/02/05/believe-it-achieve-it-five-manifestation-success-stories-16051281/

O'Malley, K. (2022, January 20). *How to manifest: A guide to willing your goals into existence in 2022.* ELLE. https://www.elle.com/uk/life-and-culture/culture/a38802302/how-to-manifest/

Olsgard, M. (2020a, February 11). *10 Signs you are out of vibrational alignment & how to fix it.* Infinite Soul Blueprint. https://www.infinitesoulblueprint.com/signs-you-are-out-of-vibrational-alignment/

Olsgard, M. (2020b, February 11). *10 Signs you are out of vibrational alignment & How to fix it.* Infinite Soul Blueprint. https://www.infinitesoulblueprint.com/signs-you-are-out-of-vibrational-alignment/

The Pennies To Millions Method to Manifest Financial Abundance. (2021, October 1). High Income Source. https://highincomesource.com/the-pennies-to-millions-method-to-manifest-financial-abundance/

Phillips, B. (n.d.). *Six ways to work with the universe to create the life you want.* Kripalu. https://kripalu.org/resources/six-ways-work-universe-create-life-you-want

Phooi, M. (2018, July 12). *12 Universal laws.* First Media Design School. https://firstmedia.edu.sg/self-development/12-universal-laws/

Prout, S. (2020, January 3). *10 Facts you need to know about manifesting.* Sarah Prout. https://sarahprout.com/10-facts-you-need-to-know-about-manifesting/

Regan, S. (2021, June 17). *The Law Of Vibration, Explained: How To Use This Universal Law To Your Advantage.* Mindbodygreen. https://www.mindbodygreen.com/articles/law-of-vibration

Regan, S. (2022, April 27). *Manifestation gets a bad rap: Allow us to explain what it really entails.* Mindbodygreen. https://www.mindbodygreen.com/articles/manifestation

Rita. (2021, September 3). *Top 4 benefits of manifestation.* The Joy Within.

https://thejoywithin.org/the-law-of-attraction/top-4-benefits-of-manifestation

Ross, C. (2022, January 21). *These celebrities predicted their futures through manifesting*. Glamour UK. https://www.glamourmagazine.co.uk/article/manifesting-celebrities

Schrijiver, K., & Schrijiver, I. (2015). Food for Thought. *Living with the Stars*, 36–51. https://doi.org/10.1093/acprof:oso/9780198727439.003.0004

Scott, E. (2020, November 18). *Understanding and using the law of attraction in your life*. verywell mind. https://www.verywellmind.com/understanding-and-using-the-law-of-attraction-3144808

Singh, A. A. (2020, October 13). *Council post: The mystery and science behind the law of attraction*. Forbes. https://www.forbes.com/sites/forbescoachescouncil/2020/10/13/the-mystery-and-science-behind-the-law-of-attraction/

Spiritual alignment: What it is & How to get it. (2018, January 25). Backpackerverse. https://backpackerverse.com/spiritual-alignment/

The Statement Scripting Method in Manifestation. (2021, October 1). High Income Source. https://highincomesource.com/the-statement-scripting-method-in-manifestation/

Stone, T. R. (2021, May 6). *How does spiritual alignment feel? See enlightening descriptions from masters*. Rose Colored Glasses. https://rosecoloredglasses.com/how-does-spiritual-alignment-feel/

The Story Scripting Method in Manifestation. (2021, October 1). High Income Source. https://highincomesource.com/the-story-scripting-method-in-manifestation/

Charbonneau, D., Consolmagno, G., Wiseman, J . (2019, February 4). *Humans in a vast universe: Astronomy and cosmic significance*. AAAS - DoSER. https://sciencereligiondialogue.org/resources/humans-in-a-vast-universe-astronomy-and-cosmic-significance/

tftd. (2017, November 3). *Keep your mind fixed on what you want in life, not on what you don't want*. The Napoleon Hill Foundation. https://www.naphill.org/tftd/thought_for_the_day_friday_november_3_2017/

Thaik, C. M. (2013, April 1). *Foods for the soul*. Psychology Today. https://www.psychologytoday.com/us/blog/the-heart/201304/foods-the-soul

The Time-Lapse Method in Manifestation. (2021, October 1). High Income Source. https://highincomesource.com/the-time-lapse-method-in-manifestation/

Wang, Y. (2016, October 5). *Between humans and the universe: All we have are the connections we make*. Northwestern. https://sites.northwestern.edu/situa tioncritical/2016/10/05/between-the-universe-and-humans-all-we-have-are-the-connections-we-make/

Warren, P., & Amir, N. (n.d.). *Law of attraction quantum physics*. EditorialTo-day.com. https://www.streetdirectory.com/etoday/law-of-attraction-quantum-physics-clpoll.html

What is the Law of Assumption and the secret behind it? (2021, December 16). Guideline Law. https://www.guidelinelaw.com/law-of-assumption/

What is the Law of Attraction? Open your eyes to a world of endless possibilities. (n.d.). The Law of Attraction. https://thelawofattraction.com/what-is-the-law-of-attraction/

Wong, K. (2020, March 18). *50 Powerful quotes from Super Attractor by Gabrielle Bernstein*. The Millennial Grind. https://millennial-grind.com/50-power ful-quotes-from-super-attractor-by-gabrielle-bernstein/

Wong, K. (2021, September 4). *How to use the law of assumption in 3 steps*. The Millennial Grind. https://millennial-grind.com/how-to-use-the-law-of-assumption-in-3-steps/

IMAGE RESOURCES

Anna Pelzer. (2017, December 7). Vegan salad bowl [Image]. Unsplash. https://unsplash.com/photos/IGfIGP5ONV0

Annie Spratt. (2021, February 6).Woman in purple dress sitting on couch [Image]. Unsplash. https://unsplash.com/photos/d_mzrEx6ytY

Dan Cristian Paduret. (2021, October 24). Photo of Dan Cristian Paduret [Image]. Unsplash. https://unsplash.com/photos/h3kuhYUCE9A

Fab Lentz. (2017, May 7). Black background with yellow text overlay [Image]. Unsplash. https://unsplash.com/photos/mRMQwK513hY

Gasbrielle Henderson. (2018, June 14). Today I am grateful book [Image]. Unsplash. https://unsplash.com/photos/M4lve6jR26E

Greg Rakozy. (2015, October 1). Silhouette photography of person [Image]. Unsplash. https://unsplash.com/photos/oMpAz-DN-9I

Hal Gatewood. (2017, October 7). Purple and pink plasma ball [Image]. Unsplash. https://unsplash.com/photos/OgvqXGL7XO4

Jasper Benning. (2019, September 30). Crystal ball photography [Image]. Unsplash. https://unsplash.com/photos/Tnk-ksP8Aqs

Kike Vega. (2018, December 9). Silhouette photography of woman doing yoga [Image]. Unsplash. https://unsplash.com/photos/F2qh3yjz6Jk

Mayur Gala. (2014, January 31). Love under setting sun [Image]. Unsplash. https://unsplash.com/photos/2PODhmrvLik

Michelle dot com. (2020, January 2021). Green plant in clear glass vase [Image]. Unsplash. https://unsplash.com/photos/ZVprbBmT8QA

Nastya Dulhier. (2018, November 16). Lighted city at night aerial photo [Image]. Unsplash. https://unsplash.com/photos/OKOOGO578eo

Paico Oficial. (2020, November 25). White printer paper besides white ceramic mug [Image]. Unsplash. https://unsplash.com/photos/7jFM-s5vzsSQ

Peter Fogden. (2018, August 13). Photo of multicolored can wall decor [Image]. Unsplash. https://unsplash.com/photos/z7oytXGI6VI

Petr Sidorov. (2021, August 1). Beautiful Tibetan singing bowl with stick [Image]. Unsplash. https://unsplash.com/photos/y0wkjVGUT9s

Sharon McCutcheon. (2018, May 14). USA dollar banknotes [Image]. Unsplash. https://unsplash.com/photos/8lnbXtxFGZw

Sivani B. (2021, June 21). 2 men playing basketball in grayscale photography [Image]. Unsplash. https://unsplash.com/photos/bczrpU9n8f4

Sixteen Miles Out. (2020, May 01). Writing in a journal [Image]. Unsplash. https://unsplash.com/photos/6Ahp8-YMoww

Vitolda Klein. (2021, March 21). Person holding black yellow red and green analog clock [Image]. Unsplash. https://unsplash.com/photos/L3zu-SWaCjSk

William Farlow. (2017, July 24). You Know Me [Image]. Unsplash. https://unsplash.com/photos/IevaZPwq0mw